INTRODUCTION
A PORT-OF-CALL

In the cold darkness before daybreak on Friday 9 September 1955 a solitary figure, dimly lit by gaslight, chalks the word LIBERTÉ upon a blackboard attached to the octagonal Customs Office at the gates of Millbay Pier. Signs of further activity are evidenced by lights in the windows of the waiting rooms nearby and the sound of shutters opening on the kiosks of Thomas Cook & Son, the Railway Booking Office and the Refreshment Bar therein. From the adjacent baggage inspection rooms the clatter of porters' trucks can be heard.

A bell rings out from a ship's telegraph aboard one of two passenger tenders which are moored at the Princess Royal Pier pontoon, next to Millbay Pier. Both ships are lit – a harsh glare from floodlights on their masts illuminates their wide, empty decks, while a warm glow shows forth from their saloon windows below. The stern rope first, then the bow rope of the tender *Sir Richard Grenville* splash into the water. The fore and aft capstans clank noisily as the ropes are hauled in, and the tender steams out into the bracing, early morning breeze and the seemingly black void of Plymouth Sound. Hundreds of gulls feeding offshore protest noisily as the tender ploughs through their midst.

First a glimmer, soon a blaze of light, the source hidden behind the silhouette of Drake's Island, attracts attention out in the Sound. In moments one of the largest passenger liners on the north Atlantic glides gracefully into view. She is lit from stem to stern, her white superstructure topped by two huge, floodlit, red funnels. On her top deck neon letters spell out her name – *Liberté*. As she anchors inside the Breakwater a small cluster of lights, which is the *Sir Richard Grenville*, attach themselves to the new arrival.

From Millbay the second tender, *Sir John Hawkins*, steams out to the French liner. Outside the gates of Millbay Pier, in Great Western Road, cars and taxis have been arriving, filling the pier approach road first and later spreading around Great Western Road to Grand Parade and the sea front. Crowd barriers are erected inside the gates as friends and relatives of the liner's passengers await the tenders' return.

The tenders SIR JOHN HAWKINS and SIR RICHARD GRENVILLE in Millbay Docks in the 1950s.

IVOR IRELAND

As the dawn sky breaks over Staddon Heights, the *Sir Richard Grenville* heads back to Millbay Docks. Crowding her decks are 225 passengers, their eyes fixed upon the striking sight of the *Liberté* – their home for the past five days since leaving New York. Aboard the second tender 227 bags of mail have been transferred from the liner, an operation supervised by Post Office staff. On the *Liberté* a temporary post desk accepts mail from the remaining passengers. The Port Health Authority's medical officer completes his documentation and departs aboard his launch. The liner is finally cleared for departure to Le Havre by Haswell & Company, the Plymouth shipping agents for the Compagnie Générale Transatlantique. In the first warming sunlight of the morning the *Liberté* weighs anchor and signals her departure with three deep blasts of her sirens and she slowly steams out of the Sound. Early morning spectators on Plymouth Hoe and the sea front continue on their way or return to Millbay Docks.

At Millbay passengers are stepping ashore from the tender, acknowledging friends on the opposite side of the barriers as they walk to the waiting rooms and Customs check. Next ashore comes the baggage, much of which sport numerous labels of trans-Atlantic and other steamship lines. Baggage and mail are transported on electric-tractor hauled trolleys, which clatter noisily over the cobbled surface.

As passengers emerge from the waiting room, their Customs formalities and baggage checks completed, a host of porters assist them, either to board the waiting railway carriages or to carry luggage to the cars of friends and rela-tives parked outside the pier gates. As the morning wears on the final obstinate trunks and suitcases are eventually secured to the last vehicles – with the knowing assistance of well practised porters.

In the full warmth of the late morning the pier returns to a lazy silence. Sunlight reflected off the shallow, emerald water, dances under the flared bows of the now dormant tenders. The name of the *Liberté* is wiped off the blackboard. Tomorrow the name *Cottica* will be written up, as the Royal Netherlands Steamship Company liner is due in from the West Indies to land 36 passengers and mail.

A similar ritual had been enacted almost daily at Millbay since the middle of the 19th century – sometimes up to five times a day. But by 1955 Plymouth's role as a mail liner port of call was drawing to a close – just eight years remained until Lloyds would list the port as closed to such traffic.

To appreciate the history of the ocean liner trade at Plymouth it is necessary to understand the rationale for the port-of-call and its continued importance almost to the very conclusion of the history of European passenger-ship line voyages.

For over a century, up to the 1960s, the world experienced a human migration from Europe, the like of which will probably never be witnessed again. During the 19th century the former European colonies of the New World expanded independently and welcomed emigrants from the other side of the Atlantic. Trade between Europe and the Americas grew accordingly. From the middle of the 19th century until the early 1920s millions of Europeans emigrated to the United States of America. Some of the most renowned shipping lines owe their origins to this migrant trade and in time these trans-Atlantic lines built some of the greatest passenger liners the world has seen – many of which called at Plymouth.

Meanwhile the European states sought new areas of influence and trade throughout the rest of the world including the African continent, India, the Far East and – initially almost exclusively for Great Britain – with the colonisation of Australia and New Zealand.

The COTTICA.
A. KITTRIDGE COLLECTION

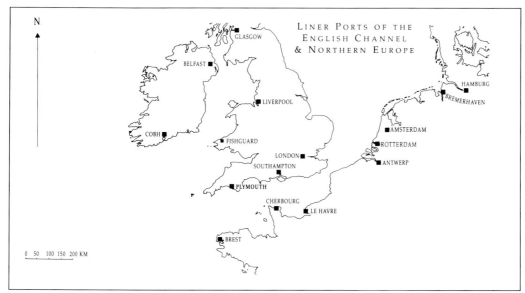

LINER PORTS OF THE ENGLISH CHANNEL & NORTHERN EUROPE

Liner ports of the English Channel and the United Kingdom.

Lines of communication were maintained by Europe's mercantile marine, protected by their respective navies. Foremost amongst these merchant and naval fleets was that of Great Britain. The British Empire was a maritime empire, totally dependent upon shipping lines established by the merchant marine to maintain trade and communications with its overseas interests. Substantial merchant fleets were also established by Germany, Holland and France. The names of many European shipping companies became synonymous with the colony or country with which they traded, developing in some cases in partnership.

The ratio of passenger and cargo accommodation available aboard colonial liners developed to meet the demands of each line's particular trade. Trans-Atlantic passenger lines were largely founded upon the emigrant trade. Even glamorous trans-Atlantic express liners of the early 20th century continued to depend upon a regular flow of emigrants packed into steerage accommodation to support extravagant building and running costs. But the most valuable and prestigious subsidy for any shipping line – vital to the economic viability of most of them – was a government mail contract, an annual subsidy to carry the mails to and from an overseas port at regular timetabled intervals.

Ever since the South Devon Railway linked the Plymouth Great Western Docks at Millbay to the railways from Bristol and London in 1850, Plymouth was specified as the ocean mail port for embarking and landing certain British Government mail contracts. The resulting Customs and Post Office facilities which were established at Millbay, together with the ocean liner expresses and travelling post offices which were run from the docks by the Great Western Railway, stimulated additional passenger and mail trade from many other European and American shipping lines.

The majority of the principal north European liner ports: Cherbourg, Le Havre, Southampton, London, Antwerp, Rotterdam, Amsterdam, Bremerhaven and Hamburg, were either located in, or reached via the English Channel. The Port of Plymouth lies at the mouth of the Channel and between 1850 and 1963 offered a convenient port-of-call for shipping lines landing passengers and mail in Britain before continuing to continental ports. It also proved expedient for liners bound for British ports to land passengers and mail at Plymouth up to a day earlier than their final destinations at Southampton, London or Liverpool.

The advantages offered by Plymouth's location and its passenger and mail facilities, attracted the world's leading lines. The port-of-call survived, and even benefitted from, various alterations in the nature of the liner trade until the 1960s, by which time passenger shipping lines had almost succumbed to airlines. There can be few, if any, ports-of-call in the world which catered for so many liners from such varied routes, for so long.

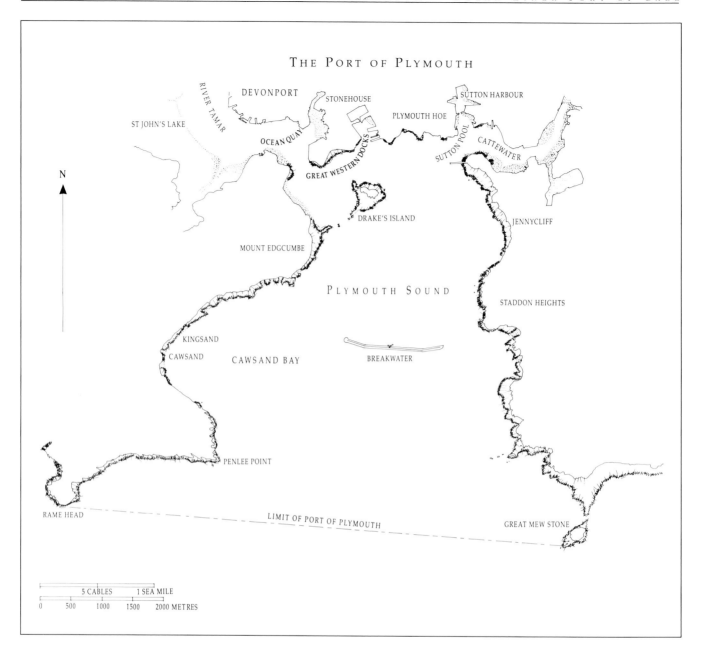

THE PORT OF PLYMOUTH

DEVONPORT

STONEHOUSE

SUTTON HARBOUR

PLYMOUTH HOE

RIVER TAMAR

ST JOHN'S LAKE

OCEAN QUAY

GREAT WESTERN DOCKS

SUTTON POOL

CATTEWATER

N

DRAKE'S ISLAND

JENNYCLIFF

MOUNT EDGCUMBE

PLYMOUTH SOUND

STADDON HEIGHTS

KINGSAND

CAWSAND

CAWSAND BAY

BREAKWATER

PENLEE POINT

RAME HEAD

LIMIT OF PORT OF PLYMOUTH

GREAT MEW STONE

5 CABLES   1 SEA MILE

0   500   1000   1500   2000 METRES

CHAPTER ONE
EMIGRANTS & OCEAN MAILS
1840 – 1877

DEVELOPMENT AS A MAILSHIP PORT-OF-CALL

It now affords us very great satisfaction to be able to state that it has definitely been arranged that the mails for the Cape of Good Hope shall be despatched from the Port of Plymouth. The vessels to be used on this service are screw steamers, of considerable power. The first of these, the *Bosphorus*, Capt. J. V. Hall, will leave Plymouth on the noon of the 15th inst and one of the company's steamers will also leave this port on the 15th of every succeeding month for the Cape, calling at Madeira and Sierra Leone.
The Plymouth and Devonport Weekly Journal
5 December 1850.

Thus was announced Plymouth's role as a port-of-call for mail and passenger steamers, having been designated as the embarkation port for the Cape Mails in the government contract which the General Screw Steam Shipping Company (GSSSCo) won earlier in the year. It was a role from which the port – and the Plymouth Great Western Docks at Millbay in particular -- was to benefit for over a century. The report concluded, rather prophetically,

…it is the commencement of a new commercial era and we do not doubt that the port will be found in all respects efficient for the service for which it is chosen.

In the event the *Bosphorus* left a day later than announced. On a wet and windy Monday morning, 16 December 1850 the Mayors, Magistrates, Aldermen and Town Councillors of Plymouth and Devonport, postal officials, military bands and sailors escorted the mails from the Post Office to Millbay Pier, where they were embarked aboard the GSSSCo's vessel. The mail comprised of seven bags; one for St Vincent, five for Sierra Leone and just one for the Cape. Thomas Gill, Chairman of the Plymouth Great Western Docks Company, was determined to publicise the event and had

called upon a few favours to secure the bands of the 4th Kings Own Regiment, the Welsh Fusiliers, the Royal Marines and *HMS Bellerophon*. He also borrowed a number of carriages to convey the entourage. The procession reformed and returned to Plymouth Guildhall where luncheon was served. Attending were dock and railway officials, directors of the GSSSCo. and officers of the *Bosphorus*, including her master, Capt. John Vine Hall. Thomas Gill said he was:

…happy to find that this glorious event had not given rise to a spirit of animosity on the part of the companies at Southampton … they could not help seeing that the extension of the steam packet system at this port would never interfere with the commerce of Southampton or prove prejudice to the interests of the companies there.

If genuine, such sentiments proved wishful, as in due course both the London & South Western Railway (L&SWR) at Southampton and the Great Western Railway (GWR) at Plymouth fought hard to secure their share of the liner trade. The competition would culminate tragically in 1906 when a speeding L&SWR Ocean Special train from Plymouth crashed at Salisbury.

THE EMIGRATION DEPOT IN SUTTON POOL

At the time of the *Bosphorus'* maiden voyage Plymouth had already been involved in the ocean passenger trade for a decade or more – as an emigration port. In the previous year 130 emigrant ships had cleared the port, bound for Australia, New Zealand and Canada. The man largely responsible both for gaining the prestigious mail trade for Millbay and establishing the emigration depot in Sutton Pool, was Thomas Gill.

During 1840 the Transportation of convicts to Australia was ended and the Colonial Land

and Emigration Commissioners offered assisted passages to the Cape, Australia and New Zealand. 'Free passage' to Australia was available for married parties up to the age of 35 years old – a £1 charge being levied 'to defray additional expenses arising from the high price of provisions, sailor's wages etc.'

Thomas Gill, Thomas Woollcombe and others formed the New Zealand Company of Plymouth in January 1840. When the Waitangi Treaty annexed New Zealand and British Sovereignty was proclaimed, later in the year, the Plymouth company sent out its first party of settlers.

The main emigrant ports in England were London, Plymouth, Bristol and Liverpool. The Colonial Land and Emigration Commissioners established Emigration Depots at the old Naval Victualling Offices at Deptford (in London) and at the Lambhay Victualling Office buildings in Plymouth's Sutton Pool.

Thomas Gill was listed as being in occupation of the Emigration Depot at Plymouth in 1845. Initially 500 emigrants could be accommodated in the depot but this was increased to 1,118 in 1883. Only poor emigrants were admitted, anyone with the means had to organise alternative lodgings while they waited for their ship. The staff included a depot master, matron, scholar, assistant, gate keeper and a house maid. It was financed by colonial land

funds in Australia. Had the Emigration Depot not existed, emigration would have continued, but no shelter would have been offered to poor emigrants.

The Irish potato famine of 1847 and the decline of the mining industry in Cornwall increased the numbers awaiting a berth to the colonies. We can only imagine the depths of despair and hardship experienced by some emigrant families as they waited forlornly, day after day at the crowded depot for their ship to arrive. At Lambhay, Lieutenant Carew R.N., the Government Emigration Agent, noted: 'High minded and religious females visit the poor on the eve of their departure from their land of birth'. These women provided clothes and offered encouragement to the emigrants. Between 1840 and 1849 over 100,000 people emigrated from the British Isles to Australia. During the 1850–59 period this increased to nearly half a million.

EMIGRANT LINES

Until the 1840s many emigrant ships were converted East Indiamen of 500 to 700 tons. Later ships were constructed specifically for the emigrant trade, many of them being chartered by Her Majesty's Colonisation Commission. In April 1844 the 628 ton *St Vincent* sailed for Sydney, offering the choice of departure from London or Plymouth. Included aboard was an unmarried females apartment – in 1840 the population of Sydney comprised 15,000 males and 4,000 females. A visitor aboard the ship noted 'many that we beheld cannot be long after their arrival without husbands'. On 16 December 1850 the *John Line*, a frigate built Indiaman of 695 tons, sailed from St Katherine's Dock, London. She called at Plymouth for settlers to the Estate of New England at Port Natal finally departing on 23 December.

As a result of an emigration boom to Australia during the 1850s, many emigrant shipping lines were established. The boom was due in part to the rush to the newly discovered gold fields of Southern Australia. On 3 February 1852 the Aberdeen Line's barque *Phoenician*, 83 days out from Sydney, landed the first major Australian gold shipment – valued at £84,000 – at Plymouth. Thus began

The ST VINCENT being towed down the River Thames from the Deptford Emigration Depot in April 1844. She called at Plymouth next, to pick up emigrants from Lambhay. Her final stop was at Cork before departing for Sydney on 16 April.
ILLUSTRATED LONDON NEWS

a long association with the 'Aberdeen Green' hulled ships of the Aberdeen Line and the start of hundreds of similar landings of specie at Plymouth from ocean liners. The Aberdeen Line's famous wool clipper, the *Samuel Plimsoll*, was a regular caller at Plymouth. On 6 August 1875 she left Plymouth with 360 emigrants aboard and ran down an Italian barque, the *Enrica*. The *Enrica*'s crew was saved and the *Samuel Plimsoll* continued on her voyage, putting into Falmouth to land the survivors.

Houlder Brothers & Company were also active in the Australian trade. Having originated as the shipping brokerage of Edwin Savory Houlder, the company started to build up their own fleet of wooden sailing ships which started calling at Plymouth in 1862.

Money Wigram & Co's fleet of 'Blackwall Frigates' were closely associated with trade to India. Once steamships started making incursions on their Indian routes the company's sailing ships were put to use in the emigrant trade. In 1861 Money Wigram & Co's steam ships were calling at Plymouth *en-route* to Melbourne. The call continued – outward and homeward bound – until 1879. Both the Aberdeen Line and Money Wigram offered accommodation for first class passengers.

In 1858 Robert Shaw and William Savill advertised 'The Passenger's Line of Packets', promoting emigration to New Zealand. The name of Shaw, Savill & Company (later Shaw, Savill & Albion) became synonymous with the development of New Zealand and the distinctive hull livery of their sailing ships – grey with a white top band and black painted ports – became a familiar feature at Plymouth. Shaw, Savill & Co.'s ports of embarkation were London's East India Dock, Gravesend, Portsmouth and Plymouth. At Plymouth the last mails were also embarked. The company continued the Plymouth call, outward and homeward bound, until 1921, latterly using Millbay's ocean passenger and mail facilities for a fortnightly mail call in both directions.

In 1873 the Immigrants Land Act provided a new spur for emigration to New Zealand by offering free passage to emigrants from the UK. In June of the same year the New Zealand Shipping Company (NZSCo.) made their first departure from Gravesend with the sailing ship *Punjab*. A decade later the NZSCo. started operating their own steamships – a requisite of obtaining a government mail contract. Their route was: London, Plymouth, Tenerife, Cape Town, Auckland and Wellington, with an occasional call at Hobart, Tasmania. The return voyage was via the Magellan Strait, calling at Buenos Aires, Tenerife, Plymouth and London. In 1884 the NZSCo. alternated their sailings with Shaw, Savill & Albion to provide a fortnightly service to New Zealand. All ships of the two companies called at Plymouth in both directions. From 1916 many of the NZSCo's voyages to New Zealand were made via the Panama Canal. The company remained faithful to the Plymouth call until 1939. A long standing tradition of the NZSCo was to register their ships at the Port of Plymouth.

From 1874 until 1887 ships of the Australian Colonial Line called in at Plymouth to pick up emigrants for Australia. The Monarch Line was in the New Zealand trade and during the 1870s and 1880s made occasional Plymouth calls for emigrants. Other lines engaged in the colonial trade to Australia and New Zealand (emigrants out – wool home) included James Beazley of Liverpool. Beazley's *Constance* sailed from Plymouth on 17 July 1850 and established a record 77 days for the voyage to Sydney. Elder & Company's *Torrens* was another famous clipper which sailed from Plymouth to Adelaide until 1891. She was one of the last sailing ships to carry passengers. Watson Brothers' two clippers, the *Ben Cruachan* and the *Ben Voirlich*, sailed regularly from Plymouth and were rivals of the Aberdeen Line's *Thermopylae* and *Samuel Plimsoll*.

The British Colonial Steamship Company started running from London's Victoria Dock to Quebec and Montreal in 1864. After Canada had gained Dominion status, the company was reorganised and renamed the Temperley Line which was 'under contract with the Dominion Government for assisted passages'. From July 1871 their steamers: *Thames, Medway, Severn* and *Niger* started calling fortnightly at Plymouth for emigrants. The call was discontinued in 1879.

Ships of the P&O, Aberdeen, Shaw Savill & Albion and White Star lines – amongst others, continued to collect emigrants from the Lambhay Depot in the last two decades of the 19th century. The depot chartered local paddle steamers to serve as tenders between Elphinstone Wharf and the ships which anchored in the Cattewater or in Plymouth Sound. Between 1862 and 1885 the passenger tug *Volunteer* of the Tamar & Tavy Steamship Co. Ltd. was regularly chartered.

Emigration from Great Britain to South Africa, Australia, New Zealand and Canada continued into the 1960s, but on an increasingly selective basis. The need of shelter for poor emigrants had diminished by the end of the 19th century and the Plymouth Emigration Depot closed. Emigrants still embarked at Plymouth, but by tender from the Plymouth Great Western Docks at Millbay.

DOCK SCHEMES AT MILLBAY C.1830–1850.

Early in the 19th century Thomas Gill was busily quarrying away the limestone bulk of Plymouth Hoe – the results of his efforts remain to be seen in the precipitous quarry face which ever since has marked the western end of Plymouth's famous headland. Virtually the whole of West Hoe, south of Cliff Road, is built upon the quarry site. Some of the limestone was destined for Gill's Soap Manufactory at Millbay and the nearby river quays of the Tamar Valley, where it was burnt in limekilns and used to dress the soil of local farms. To facilitate shipment of this limestone by river barges a cut, or canal, was made from the adjacent Millbay into the quarry area.

Another, more substantial, dock development was built in Millbay during the 1830s on the site of the old tide mill, in the north eastern corner of Millbay. Named Union Dock it was owned by Richard and David Derry and James Meadows Rendel. Rendel was a distinguished civil engineer who was establishing a reputation for his riverine, dock and waterfront projects. The dock comprised of a pier, wharves and warehouses on the Millbay waterfront, with a small inner basin reclaimed from part of the former marshland once known as the Sourpool, on the north side of Millbay Road.

Gill obtained an Act of Parliament in 1840 to improve his own docking facilities by building a pier at the entrance to Millbay. The Act protected the rights of the Union Dock and James Rendel was appointed to construct the pier. Nathaniel Beardmore supervised the works for Rendel, who introduced a system of building high stages over the pier works from which the foundation rubble was dropped into the water – in the case of Millbay some 38 feet deep. Millbay Pier was completed in 1844 and was 500 feet long. The pier was strengthened

The small jetty at Sandy Cove in Millbay c. 1830, showing Drake's Island, Mount Edgcumbe and in the distance Penlee Point.

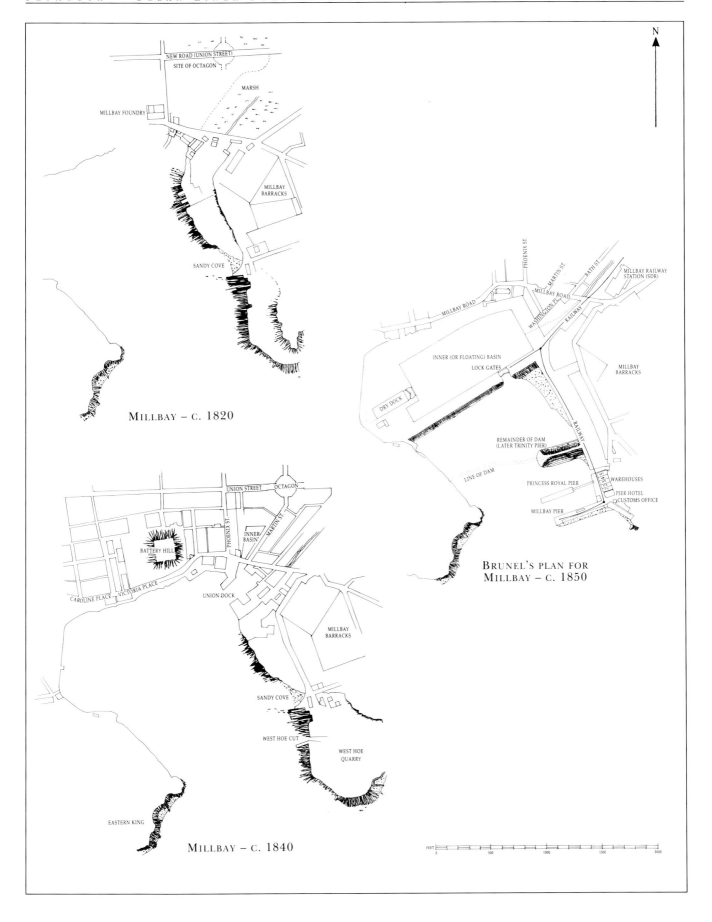

N

MILLBAY – C. 1820

BRUNEL'S PLAN FOR
MILLBAY – C. 1850

MILLBAY – C. 1840

by I. K. Brunel during the 1850s and lengthened in a programme of dock works during 1903.

During 1845 the steamship *Great Britain* berthed at Millbay Pier and was opened to the public. The visit of Brunel's ship offered publicity for the promoters of the South Devon Railway (SDR) – of which Gill was the Chairman and Brunel the Engineer. The SDR was to link Plymouth to London via the lines of the Bristol & Exeter and the Great Western railways. Gill, understandably, favoured a dock development and rail link at Millbay. Brunel meanwhile drew up alternative plans for the railway to link with Sutton Harbour, on the eastern side of Plymouth Hoe. The promoters of this alternative venture included Thomas Woollcombe, who later succeeded Gill as Chairman of the SDR. However, in July 1846 the Admiralty announced its refusal of permission for the Sutton Harbour and Dock Company to convert the harbour into a floating dock, as lock gates would compromise Sutton Harbour's status as a harbour of refuge. No objections were raised concerning a dock development in Millbay.

Thomas Gill and others formed the Plymouth Great Western Dock Company and assisted by Gill, who was Member of Parliament for Plymouth 1841–46, obtained an Act of Parliament – the Plymouth Great Western Dock Act 1846. The Act empowered the new company to purchase the existing harbour works from Thomas Gill, to build an inner basin and provide a dry dock. A further Act, the Great Western Dock (Amendment) Act 1848, authorised further capital. But more importantly, the GWR, the Bristol and Exeter Railway (B&ER) and the SDR were each authorised to subscribe specified sums and empowered to appoint directors: one each by the GWR and B&ER, and two by the SDR. I. K. Brunel was appointed as Engineer for the dock works. The Union Dock disappeared under the new, larger development – David Derry, one of the Union Dock's owners, became Deputy Chairman of the SDR.

OVERSEAS MAIL

During the 1830s overseas mail was carried either as 'ship's letters' – the sender designating the ship or shipping line on the envelope or package, or by Post Office mail packets. Owing to its huge, natural, safe anchorage for sailing vessels and convenient position at the mouth of the English Channel, Falmouth had been designated as the Post Office Packet port for the (Iberian) Peninsular mails since 1688. The West Indies and North American mails followed in the 1750s and the Mediterranean and South American mails in the early 1800s. The Cornish port became famous for its Post Office sailing packets and as the port for orders for many of the sailing ships in the Western Approaches. In 1837 the Admiralty was charged with arranging future packet contracts with private shipping lines wherever possible, with the Post Office and Treasury specifying the terms of the contract. In 1840 Admiralty commissioners visited British ports to assess their individual merits as mail ports. The need to reorganise the system of carriage of overseas mail was necessitated by the increasing availability of rail transport and ocean going steamships – both of which were introducing speed and regularity previously unknown.

The criteria for a successful mail port changed accordingly to include a safe anchorage or docking facility for steamships and a railway connection. In 1840 the North American mails were transferred from Falmouth to Liverpool, the new contract having been won by Samuel Cunard's British & North American Royal Mail Steam Packet Company. Samuel Cunard gained the contract against the rival bids of the St George Steam Packet Company and the Bristol based Great Western Steamship Company – Brunel's grand plan for extending the Great Western route across the Atlantic. Until 1843 Falmouth remained as the packet port for the Royal Mail Steam Packet Company's (RMSPCo.) West Indian contract and the Peninsular & Oriental Steam Navigation Company's (P&O) Peninsular and Mediterranean contracts. A railway connection to Falmouth, however, was to be a further twenty years in arriving. Sailing packets from Falmouth continued carrying the South American mails until December 1850, owing to difficulties encountered in establishing suitable coaling stations for steamships. In 1860 the Post Office became responsible for awarding mail contracts.

Thomas Allom's engraving of Plymouth Breakwater under construction in the 1830s. Granite and limestone blocks from Oreston were taken out to the Breakwater aboard specially built vessels – like that shown on the left. The Breakwater was completed in 1841. Thus protected Plymouth's foreshore was suitable for developments such as Thomas Gill's plans for Millbay.

At Plymouth the requirement for safe anchorage was satisfied in 1841 with the completion of the 5,000 feet long Breakwater in Plymouth Sound. Engineered by John Rennie and Joseph Whidbey and commenced in 1812, the Breakwater offered a substantial, safe, deep water anchorage and in turn protected the previously exposed Millbay, enabling Thomas Gill to construct his pier, which offered docking facilities for the early mailships. The SDR's Plymouth terminus was opened in 1849. The station site was adjacent to the north east corner of Millbay and a line was extended to link with the Great Western Docks' own rails during the following year. The rail linked dock facilities that Gill had been instrumental in establishing at Millbay were granted Customs facilities in 1850. In the same year the Customs Office – a distinctive, three storeyed, octagonal, limestone building – was designed by James Rendel's close friend, George Wightwick and built at the gates of Millbay Pier. Later in the year the Pier Hotel was built on the opposite side of the gates.

A Select Parliamentary Committee Report in 1849 advised that, in future, mail contracts should be awarded to steamship companies in open competition. In 1850, having fulfilled the criteria for a mail port and being admirably located for the purpose, Plymouth was desig-nated as embarkation port for the Cape Mails and, as described above, the GSSSCo. won the contract to carry the mails.

THE PLYMOUTH GREAT WESTERN DOCKS

The floating basin of the Plymouth Great Western Docks was opened in February 1857 and measured 1,200 feet x 500 feet. A dry dock was opened in the same year. A dam had been constructed across Millbay to protect the inner harbour works. The greater part of this dam was removed upon completion of the work, but the eastern end was retained to form the foundation of a new pier. The pier became known as Trinity Pier, as it was originally used to accommodate Trinity House warehouses – for the maintenance of the Eddystone and other lighthouses. Trinity Pier was enlarged in 1878 and was used to land ocean mails. A third pier was also built between Millbay Pier and what was to become Trinity Pier. Named the Princess Royal Pier it comprised of a short limestone abutment, a length of decking carried on cylindrical iron piers and a large 300 feet long x 40 feet wide floating pontoon. The pontoon, which appears on Brunel's original plans for the dock works, was originally built in 1852 for bunkering ships of the Irish Steamship Company and was designed to hold 4000 tons of coal. In common with Trinity Pier, the Princess Royal Pier

George Wightwick's octagonal Customs Office of 1850. Photographed in 1988.
                                            A. KITTRIDGE

Two photographs taken in 1987 provide a panoramic view of the entrance to Millbay Pier. From the left: the wall of the Customs Office, Millbay Pier gates, the Pier Hotel building and the five warehouses which date from the 1850s. The first two warehouses were converted as waiting rooms. The remaining three had three storeys opening onto the road and four storeys on the sea-ward side – the extra basement floor being the baggage inspection rooms.

A. KITTRIDGE

was used in the ocean liner trade, mainly as moorings for the tenders and for use by the tenders' excursion passengers. In 1891 East Quay was covered with a railway style awning, which extended from the Princess Royal Pier to Millbay Pier – linking with a similar covering which already existed over a part of Millbay Pier.

The dock works were severely damaged in a storm in October 1857. The substantial repair bill revealed the precarious finances of the dock company, which was unable to meet the cost of repair and failed to pay arrears of interest to Preference Shareholders. The Plymouth Great Western Dock Act 1858 gave the SDR the power to provide financial guarantees and,

The arrival of the dock company's first tender, the SIR FRANCIS DRAKE, announced in the Western Morning News June 1873.

PLYMOUTH GREAT WESTERN DOCKS.

THE NEW AND POWERFUL IRON-BUILT
PADDLE STEAMER

SIR FRANCIS DRAKE

Specially constructed for attending on

THE WEST INDIA MAIL

And other Ocean Steamers,

And to Meet the General Requirements of the **PORT OF PLYMOUTH**, is expected to arrive This Day.

This vessel has been designed to combine speed and safety, with ample deck and cabin accommodation for Sea and River Excursions.

With a view to her use as a POWERFUL TUG, she has been fitted with a pair of diagonal disconnecting engines, capable of working at over 500-horse power.

The trial trips have resulted most satisfactorily, and the officers of the Board of Trade have formally approved of the vessel for all purposes.

In addition to the Local Excursions in which the **SIR FRANCIS DRAKE** will be employed soon after arrival, it is proposed to make occasional trips to the **CHANNEL ISLANDS** and elsewhere.

For further particulars apply to

J. ROONEY, Secretary.

June 24th, 1873.

---

more importantly, the dock company was empowered to sell or lease the docks to the SDR after seven years.

Due in part to the increased size of mail-ships and the ever present need for speed in embarking and disembarking mails, it became expedient for them to anchor in Plymouth Sound and be attended by a boat from Millbay. Until 1873 the Great Western Docks chartered local paddle steamers as tenders. These steamers included the tug *Secret*, the passenger/tug *Volunteer* and the River Tamar passenger steamer *Fairy*. Early in 1872 consideration was given by the dock company to acquiring their own tender and an order was placed with William Allsup's Caledonian Works in Preston for an iron paddle steamer. She was delivered on 24 June 1873 and the Great Western Docks Company announced her arrival in the *Western Morning News*, stating that she had been '…Specially constructed for attending on the West India Mail (contracted to the RMSPCo.) and other ocean steamers'. She was named the *Sir Francis Drake*, establishing a nomenclature of Westcountry seamen that was to be carried by Millbay's liner tender fleet until 1963. The *Sir Francis Drake* measured 173 tons gross, 131.3 feet long x 20.1 feet wide x 10 feet deep. Amongst the passenger certificates she held was a Class IV (semi smooth water – for tendering in Plymouth Sound and Cawsand Bay) for 352 passengers (summer) and 251 (winter).

To negate the need for chartering local

steamboats to assist the *Sir Francis Drake* in attending mailboats and passenger liners a second tender was ordered in 1876. Named the *Sir Walter Raleigh*, she was an iron paddle steamer, built by William Allsup. Her passenger numbers for tendering were 250 (summer) and 177 (winter). Initially passengers were charged 6d (2½p) for landing by tender at Plymouth – inclusive of all baggage, but later the costs were transferred to the relevant shipping line.

Negotiations for the sale of the docks to the SDR began in 1873 and under the conditions of the South Devon Railway Act 1874, ownership of the Plymouth Great Western Docks were vested in the SDR, B&ER and GWR. The railway companies managed the docks with a Joint Committee chaired by Daniel Gooch.

In 1878 the interests of the SDR and the B&ER were transferred to the GWR by the Great Western Railway and South Devon Railway Companies Amalgamation Act of 1878. The entire mainline from London to Plymouth, and Millbay Docks were now under the control of the GWR.

MAIL STEAMSHIP LINES

The origins of most of the great passenger ship lines of the twentieth century are found with their earliest mail contracts. These origins also account for the establishment of a Plymouth call by some of them, being either compulsory or expedient to gaining the contract. The mail handling facility which had been established at Millbay was instrumental in winning most of the nineteenth century line calls. By and large this remained the case throughout the history of line calls at Plymouth, although other factors combined to contribute to the continued attraction of the port-of-call.

In addition to winning the Cape mail contract in 1850, the GSSSCo. also gained an Indian mail contract and established a passenger service to Australia. However, in 1852 it was the Australian Royal Mail Steam Navigation Company (Australian RMSNCo.) which was awarded a contract to carry the Australian mails via the Cape. Plymouth was designated as the packet station for the Australian mail, and the company's steamship, the *Australian*, departed

Millbay in 1872. West Hoe quarry is on the left. Opposite Trinity Pier is a rocky outcrop which was used to form part of the dam for the Inner Basin works. The rocks were nicknamed 'Brunel's Rocks', the engineer having been compelled to leave them through lack of funds for their removal. As a consequence ships had to navigate the restricted channel between the rocks and Trinity Pier. Two ships came to grief on the rocks. As a result of the second accident in 1879, when the steamer SHADWAN was temporarily stranded, the dock company arranged for the removal of the rocks by blasting.
A battery once occupied the high cliff behind North Quay. Later a fever hospital was established there. The limestone cliff belonged to the Earl of Mt Edgcumbe and was gradually quarried away.
DETAIL FROM ILLUSTRATED LONDON NEWS PANORAMA OF PLYMOUTH

The African Steamship Company's FORERUNNER.

on her maiden voyage from London on 29 May 1852, calling in at Plymouth for the mails. Unfortunately, the *Australian* hit Millbay Pier and was damaged, requiring repairs at Devonport Dockyard before she could continue. Her fleet sister, the *Sydney*, commenced running on 31 July. The *Australian* took forty-eight days to reach the Cape and ninety-five to reach Sydney. The *Sydney* performed little better. The company's third departure, the *Melbourne*, fared much worse, taking seventy-seven days just to reach the Cape. The company's steamer *Adelaide* was another visitor to Devonport Dockyard during the following December, needing a replacement rudder fitted. By 1854 the Australian RMSNCo. was experiencing difficulty in maintaining the contract. Their problems were compounded in March 1854 when the *Australian* grounded in Table Bay and the mails had to be carried to Australia by the Royal Navy. Although the *Australian* was refloated, the Admiralty had had enough and effectively ended the contract by requisitioning the company's ships to serve as troopships to Crimea.

The Australian Auxiliary Steam Clipper Company briefly ran an Australian service between 1856-1858. Their steamers *Istamboul* and *Indomitable* called at Plymouth.

During the 1850's there was considerable debate over the best route for the Australian mails. P&O, which had already briefly held an Australian contract, adopted a flexible approach in attempting to accommodate the government's requirements, but opinion was against further expansion of P&O's subsidised

monopoly east of Suez. The contract was awarded to the European & Australian Royal Mail Company which, like the Australian RMSNCo. before, proved incapable of fulfilling the contract. P&O eventually gained the contract in 1859.

McGregor Laird founded the African Steamship Company in 1852 – 'for the conveyance of cargo and passengers and the carriage of the mails to the west coast of Africa'. The company's first sailing was on 24 September 1852, when the *Forerunner* departed from London, calling at: Plymouth, Madeira, Tenerife, Bathurst (Gambia) and Freetown (Sierra Leone).

The London agents of the African Steamship Company were Alexander Elder and John Dempster. From 1868 they also managed the British & African Steamship Company. The name of Elder Dempster became synonymous with the development of west African ports and trade. Ships of Elder Dempsters' lines were calling at Plymouth from the earliest days until 1939.

Southampton was chosen as a terminus port and base by the GSSSCo., P&O and the RMSPCo. Although the L&SWR line was open throughout between Southampton and London in May 1840, the Admiralty insisted on continuing Falmouth's designation as the packet port for both the P&O's and the RMSPCo's mail contracts. In July 1843, when the docks at Southampton were fully opened, the Admiralty relented and the two companies established their termini there. In the same year the Union Steam Collier Company was established to satisfy the resulting increase in demand for coal at the port, being contracted to supply all three of the above named mailboat companies. In 1856 the Union Steam Collier Company was renamed the Union Steam Ship Company (Union SSCo.) and tendered for the mail contract to Cape Colony and Natal – the GSSSCo. having withdrawn their Cape and Indian passenger and mail services in 1854. The Union SSCo. subsequently won the contract to maintain monthly sailings to the Cape and their steamship, the *Dane*, departed from Southampton on 15th September 1857, calling at Plymouth for the mails. The voyage to the

Cape took 44 days. In the next month the Union SSCo's *Celt* embarked upon the second sailing. And in November the *Norman* completed the third trip in 37 days. The steamers called at Plymouth outward and homeward – the *Dane* made her first return call to Plymouth on 6 January 1858. Calls by the Union SSCo's mailships ceased during 1877, until briefly resumed in 1893, but the company's intermediate ships continued to call until 1900. The Union SSCo. and other mailboat lines provided extra sailings in between their scheduled mailboat departures, which became known as intermediate sailings. The Union SSCo. established an intermediate sailing in 1863 from Southampton to Port Elizabeth, calling at Plymouth and Cape Town.

The Hamburg Amerikanische Paketfahrt Aktien Gesellschaft (HAPAG) or Hamburg American Line in English speaking countries, was formed in 1847, principally to carry emigrants from Hamburg to New York aboard their fleet of sailing ships. In 1856 the company started operating steamships on the route, and in the following year inaugurated an intermediate call at Southampton for passengers and mails. When alterations were made to the terms of the British mail contract in 1868, HAPAG decided not to apply for renewal and withdrew the Southampton call. Plymouth, Havre and Cherbourg were substituted as westbound and eastbound ports-of-call. The Southampton westbound call was re-introduced in 1889, but Plymouth remained as the eastbound port of call. With the exception of the years 1904–1906, when Dover was unsuccessfully substituted as the British port-of-call for all their services, HAPAG's Atlantic liners continued calling at Plymouth until 1914. Initially only their New York mailboats called, but in the 1870's the company's intermediate New York steamers and West Indies/South American services were using the port.

The 1870s heralded a substantial increase in the number of lines using Plymouth as a port of call. The commencement of the NZSCo's Plymouth call in 1872 was noted above. In October of the same year the steamship *Rotterdam* called at Plymouth on her maiden voyage between Rotterdam and New York. Owned by Plate, Reuchlin & Co., the *Rotterdam* was soon joined by a sister ship, the *Maas*, and together they maintained a monthly trans-Atlantic service. In the following year a new company was formed to take over the line and provide new capital. The Nederlandsch–Amerikaansche Stoomvaart Maatschappij (NASM), known in English speaking countries as the Holland America Line, was incorporated on 18 April 1873. The *Rotterdam* and the *Maas* continued as before and were joined in 1874 by two new ships, the *P. Carland* and the *W. A. Scholten*. The new steamers carried more passengers (50 cabin, 600 steerage) and cut the crossing time from Plymouth to New York by two days – to twelve days and four hours. Within a short time of the new ships coming into service the Plymouth call was dropped. The company was not to return until weekly east and westbound calls were resumed in 1910.

In 1873 Plymouth played host to a second Hamburg based trans-Atlantic line, the Deutsche Transatlantische Dampfschiffahrts Gesellschaft – known as the Eagle Line in Great Britain and the United States, and the Adler Linie in Germany, from the eagle depicted on its houseflag. The company dispatched the 3,500 tons gross steamer *Goethe* on her maiden voyage from Hamburg to New York in 1873. The *Goethe* made her first Plymouth call on her return trip in September. A Plymouth call was subsequently made on each eastbound voyage. By 1875 the Eagle Line was operating seven steamers on the route but on the night of 7 May their steamship, the *Schiller*, en-route from New York to Plymouth with 254 passengers, 101 crew, $300,000 of specie, and Australian

The Eagle Line's ill fated trans-Atlantic liner, SCHILLER. Due at Plymouth from New York, she was wrecked in the Isles of Scilly on 7 May 1875 with the loss of 311 lives.

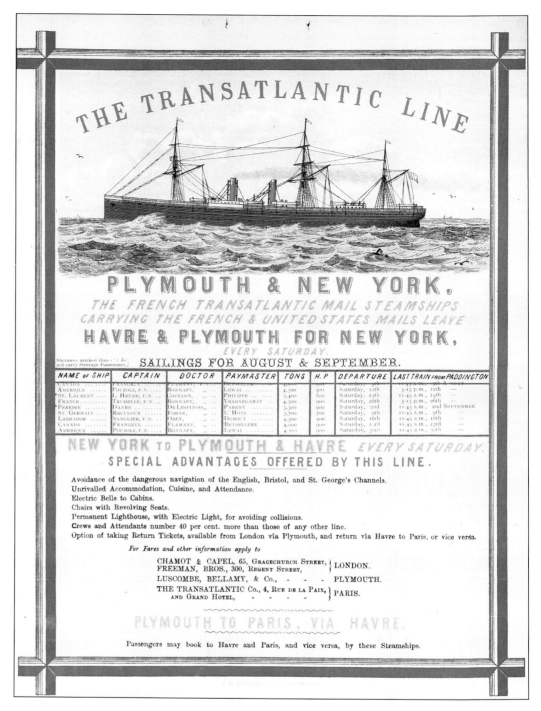

CGT's poster and timetable for
August and September 1876.
POST OFFICE ARCHIVES

and New Zealand mails aboard, was wrecked on the Retarrier Ledges in the Isles of Scilly. She struck the reef in fog at low tide and the rising water, crashing over the reef and stranded liner, swept many into the sea. Of 355 passengers and crew, 311 were killed. Only two of the ship's eight boats survived to reach the Island of Tresco. The Eagle Line subsequently fared badly during a slump in German shipping and sold their entire fleet and business to

HAPAG, their principal rival at Hamburg.

A line which was to prove more durable also commenced calls in 1873. The Royal Mail Steam Packet Company was incorporated by Royal Charter in 1839,

> …for the conveyance of the mails to and from Great Britain and the West India Islands and North and South America and other foreign ports and for that purpose to establish a regular supply of steam and other vessels…

Southampton was chosen as the home port but, as previously noted, until 1843 the mails were to be delivered and collected at Falmouth – mail coaches being required to link Falmouth to the nearest rail-head. In 1851 the RMSPCo. commenced direct services to South America, initially to Rio de Janeiro and later to Montevideo and Buenos Aires. Calls were instituted at Plymouth and some Continental ports in 1873. When the RMSPCo. lost the West Indian mail contract in 1905 their liners stopped calling at Plymouth.

The Peninsular Steam Navigation Company gained the Government contract to carry the Gibraltar mails in 1837, adding the Egypt mail contract two years later. In 1840 the Peninsular Steam Navigation Company was renamed the Peninsular & Oriental Steam Navigation Company, being incorporated by Royal Charter. An Indian mail contract (to Ceylon and Calcutta) was awarded in the same year. To fulfil the terms of the contract P&O maintained one line of steamers operating between Southampton and Alexandria and a second running between Suez and India. The complete journey from Britain to India by this route became famous as the Overland Route. In 1845 P&O extended services to Singapore and Hong Kong.

The opening of de Lesseps' Suez Canal in 1869 signalled a gradual change in P&O's operation, their steamers being able to make the complete voyage. The company's ships began to load cargo in London during 1874, calling at Southampton for passengers and mail – some calls were also made at Plymouth. By 1881 the mails (excepting the Gibraltar mail) were going overland across Europe by rail via the Italian port of Brindisi. The passenger terminus was moved to London and Southampton was dropped as a port of call. Southampton's loss was Plymouth's gain and from 1881 until 1939 all of P&O's liners, from India, Australia and the Far East, made a homeward call at the port, landing passengers and the Gibraltar mail.

The origins of the Compagnie Générale Transatlantique (CGT) – also known as the French Line – date back to 1854. The company commenced West Indies and Central American services in 1862 with four steamers. In the same year eight steamers were placed on an express passenger/mail service between Havre and New York. An intermediate service was added later. CGT introduced a Plymouth call in December 1875. Unfortunately the passenger figures proved disappointing and in 1878 the Plymouth call was withdrawn. Forty four years were to elapse before CGT returned to Plymouth and established a regular call that was to survive into the 1960s.

The increase in the numbers of mailboat and emigration lines using Plymouth as a port of call during the 1870's, was completed in 1877, when in June, August and September respectively, the steamships *Lusitania*, *Chimborazo* and the *Cuzco*, under charter to the Orient Line, departed from London for Melbourne and Sydney, embarking passengers by tender at Gravesend and Plymouth. The origins of the Orient Line lay with the London ship-broking firm of Anderson, Anderson & Company who since 1853 owned the full rigged ship *Orient*, running to Australia. The *Orient*'s first departure from Plymouth was on 5 July 1856. In 1874 the company laid the foundations of their steamship service with two voyages to Australia, the first by the auxiliary steamship *Easby* and the second by the screw steamship *St Osyth*, which called at Plymouth. In conjunction with Frederick Green & Company; Anderson, Anderson & Company next chartered from the Pacific Steam Navigation Company the steamers *Lusitania*, *Chimborazo*, *Cuzco* and the *Garronne* to establish a regular Australian service. The *Lusitania* departed from Plymouth on 28 June 1877, reaching Melbourne in 40 days. The return to Plymouth from Adelaide, via the Suez Canal was made in 41 days. With the success of the sailings the Orient Steam Navigation Company was formed in the following year to purchase the four steamers. The Company's ships continued to call at Plymouth until 1939

For emigrant and mail lines to Australia, New Zealand, South Africa and Canada, the Plymouth call was usually a contractual requirement. For the trans-Atlantic lines Plymouth's passenger and mail handling facilities and geographical position offered an attractive and efficient port of call in the British Isles. Although HAPAG alone amongst trans-Atlantic lines was calling in 1880, a gradual change in the nature of the north Atlantic passenger trade towards the end of the 19th century encouraged more north European lines to introduce a Plymouth call, it being the most conveniently positioned British mail port to the Continent. Quite simply it was quicker for Continental lines to land passengers and mails for Britain at Plymouth rather than at Southampton. Likewise for the P&O and Orient lines and later a growing number of other British lines, Plymouth offered their passengers the advantage of saving a day in reaching London or Liverpool, or indeed of avoiding those cities altogether.

Bristol & Exeter Railway timetable 1877.
A. Stephen & Son – listed under the owners column – is possibly Alexander Stephen of Glasgow, a shipbuilder who built clippers for the colonial trade, including, in the 1870s, ships for the New Zealand Shipping Co. and Shaw, Savill & Co. Also making Plymouth calls at the same time were Thomas Stephens & Sons, who ran a renowned wool clipper, the THOMAS STEPHENS, *to Melbourne.*

MICHAEL MESSENGER COLLECTION

BRISTOL AND EXETER RAILWAY. 25

PLYMOUTH.

Arrangements for the Departure of Mail and Passenger Ships.

JANUARY, 1877.

JAN.	Ports of destination.	Ship.	Owners.
1	Melbourne	Somersetshire	M. Wigram & Sons
1	Havre and Hamburgh	Saxonia	Hamburgh American Company
5	Cape of Good Hope	American	Union Steamship Company
6	New York	France	French Transatlantic Company
7	Cherbourg and Hamburgh	Pommerania	Hamburgh American Company
7	Antwerp and Bremen	Habsburg	North German Lloyds
8	Adelaide	British Enterprise	British Ship Owners' Company
9	Havre	Labrador	French Transatlantic Company
12	Port Elizabeth (Algoa Bay)	Asiatic	Union Steamship Company
13	Cherbourg and Southampton	Don	Royal Mail Steam Packet Company
14	Cherbourg and Hamburgh	Suevia	Hamburgh American Company
14	London	Courland	Donald Currie and Co.
19	Cape of Good Hope	Anglian	Union Steamship Company
20	New York	Labrador	French Transatlantic Company
21	Havre and Hamburgh	Rhenania	Hamburgh American Company
21	Cherbourg and Hamburgh	Lessing	Hamburgh American Company
22	Sydney	Earl Dalhousie	A. Stephen and Son
23	Havre	Canada	French Transatlantic Company
27	Melbourne	Durham	M. Wigram and Son
28	London	Edinburgh Castle	Donald Currie and Co.
29	Cherbourg and Southampton	Para	Royal Mail Steam Packet Company

Arrangements for the Arrival of Mails and Passenger Ships.

JAN.	Whence.	Ship.	Owners.
1	West Indies	Saxonia	Hamburgh American Company
7	New York	Pommerania	Do. do.
7	Brazils and Lisbon	Habsburg	North German Lloyds
8	Cape of Good Hope	African	Union Steamship Company
9	New York	Labrador	French Transatlantic Company
13	West Indies, &c.	Don	Royal Mail Packet Company
14	New York	Suevia	Hamburgh American Company
14	Cape of Good Hope	Courland	Donald Currie & Company
21	West Indies	Rhenania	Hamburgh American Company
21	New York	Lessing	Do. do.
22	Port Elizabeth (Algoa Bay)	Syria	Union Steamship Company
23	New York	Canada	French Transatlantic Company
28	Cape of Good Hope	Edinburgh Castle	Donald Currie & Company
29	West Indies	Para	Royal Mail Packet Company

The Company does not hold itself responsible for the correctness of this information although every care is taken to procure it.

LOCAL AGENTS.

Hamburg American Company—SMITH, SUNDIUS & Co., Millbay Road, Plymouth.
Australian Colonial Line   "   "   "
Allan Line —SMITH, SUNDIUS & Co.
Royal Mail Packet Company—FOX, SONS & Co., Plymouth.
Canadian and Australian Lines—W. T. WEEKES & Co., Barbican, Plymouth.
Union Steamship Company Limited—H. J. WARING, Millbay.
Netherlands American Company—H. S. ROBERTS & Co., Parade, Plymouth.
Passengers arriving by the Ocean Steamers at Plymouth, and booking through from there or Falmouth to Paddington, may break their journey at Exeter or Bristol, and their Tickets will be available for thirty days.

The paddle steamer *Sir Walter Raleigh* was sold four years later, as a tug to a South Shields owner. By 1896 the *Sir Francis Drake* was only certificated during the summer months when she was mainly employed on excursions.

HOTELS AND PASSENGER ACCOMMODATION

The Gothic styled Duke of Cornwall Hotel was built at a cost of £40,000 in 1862. Situated directly opposite Millbay Station, it was owned by the Plymouth Hotel Company, subscribers to which included directors of the railway companies. The circular tower on the western end of the hotel offered panoramic views of both Plymouth Sound and Millbay and might have originally served as a lookout, forewarning the hotel and catering staff of a liner's arrival. The hotel provided catering services aboard the GWR's liner tenders and in the waiting rooms of the Pier Hotel building. Two other hotels were opened soon after, just yards away from the Duke of Cornwall, these were the Continental Hotel and the adjacent Albion Hotel – which in 1904 was taken over by the Continental.

In 1880 the Pier Hotel at Millbay was leased to the Plymouth Hotel Company which was to improve the waiting room accommodation for liner passengers and operate a refreshment room. The upper floors of the hotel building were converted to offices for shipping agents and consulates, while the ground floor was linked with the two adjacent warehouses to provide an enlarged waiting room area and

The Waiting Room at Millbay c. 1906.
DOUGLASS HOPPINS COLLECTION

The SIR FRANCIS DRAKE pictured steaming into Salcombe Harbour on an excursion in 1896.
NATIONAL MARITIME MUSEUM

booking offices. The western facing limestone exteriors of the two warehouses were rendered to match the hotel building. The complete group of five warehouses on East Quay were all specified on Brunel's initial works drawings and built between 1850–57. The three other warehouses were three and a half storeyed buildings. Their ground floors were each linked with large sliding doors and were employed as the baggage inspection rooms. Their first floors opened out at the back directly onto Great Western Road at road level. As the number of passengers landing at Millbay increased a baggage railway was laid out on Millbay Pier, running around to East Quay and inside the baggage inspection rooms.

NEW LINE CALLS

In the decade up to the turn of the century a number of important lines inaugurated Plymouth calls. The British India Steam Navigation Co. Ltd. (BI), was based in Calcutta, and maintained a network of lines east of Suez, including Indian coastal services and mail steamers to the Far East. With the opening of the Suez Canal an India–UK main line was

The MORAVIAN, *of the Aberdeen Line, in Cawsand Bay on 9 April 1907. The Breakwater lighthouse is in the background.*
SYDNEY GOODMAN COLLECTION

established. Later a through service between UK and east Africa was introduced. A separate company, British India Associated Steamers (BIAS), was created to manage those BI lines which operated from the UK. In 1881 BIAS gained a mail contract from the Queensland Government to carry the mails direct from the UK to Brisbane, via the Torres Strait. Titled the Queensland Royal Mail Line it was the longest shipping contract in the world. From commencement until 1895, when the service was withdrawn, ships of the Queensland Royal Mail Line called at Plymouth homeward (UK) bound. In addition to the Queensland steamers BIAS ships on the UK–Suez–Colombo–Madras–Calcutta route were also calling in at Plymouth homeward bound. In 1903 British India Associated Steamers Ltd was wound up and all the steamers were transferred to BI. In 1914 P&O and BI amalgamated but each company retained their individual trade and identities. BI liners on the Calcutta and Bombay routes and later, those from the east African services, continued to call in at Plymouth, homeward, until the 1950s.

The sailing ships of the Aberdeen Line had been calling at Plymouth since the 1850s. The line's first steamship, the *Aberdeen*, entered service in 1881. In the following year a steamship service was introduced from London to Melbourne, Sydney and Brisbane, via the Cape, with a Plymouth call in each direction.

In 1884 the Oceanic Steam Navigation Company's (White Star Line) liners *Ionic, Doric* and *Coptic* inaugurated the White Star/Shaw Savill & Albion Joint Service from London to Wellington – whereby White Star provided the ships and crew, while SS&A managed the venture. The service lasted for sixty years and calls were made at Plymouth both outward and homeward. From London liners of the Joint Service called at Plymouth, Tenerife, Cape Town, Hobart, Wellington, Napier, and returned – Montevideo, Rio de Janeiro, Tenerife, Plymouth and London. The *Gothic* was built for the trade in 1893, followed by the *Delphic* in 1897. The *Athenic, Corinthic* and a new *Ionic* were built for the joint service in 1901–2.

Some excitement was caused on 7 June

The White Star Line's PERSIC *steaming into Plymouth Sound.*
SYDNEY GOODMAN COLLECTION

1906 when the *Gothic* arrived from Wellington with a fire in her cargo of wool. A GWR tender took off passengers and mail and the *Gothic* was towed into the shallow Cattewater and grounded in Clovelly Bay, off Turnchapel. The fire was brought under control during the following day and the *Gothic* was pumped out, re-floated and towed back into Plymouth Sound.

In 1914 outbound calls of the Joint Service were made at Southampton and the Plymouth call reduced to homebound only. Southampton replaced Plymouth both out and home in 1921. White Star also started an Australian service in 1899 with the steamships: *Afric, Medic* and *Persic*. The *Runic* and *Suevic* were introduced on the service in 1901. A homebound call was made at Plymouth.

Steamers of the National Line ran between Liverpool and New York and additionally, from 1870, between London and New York. In 1884 some of the National Line's London steamers began calling at Plymouth on the outward voyage. But when the passenger service from London was withdrawn in the following year, so too was the Plymouth call.

Since 1872 the Cape liners of Donald Currie & Co. had run from London, providing a passenger and private mail service. A call was made at Dartmouth to collect mail. The service was originally advertised in Britain as the Colonial Line. Four years later Donald Currie incorporated the Castle Mail Packets Co. Ltd. (known as the Castle Line) – most of his steamers being named with a castle suffix. In the same year the Colonial Government of South Africa awarded the Union SSCo. and the Castle Line a joint mail contract. Castle

Line steamers introduced an intermediate call at Plymouth to pick up and land mail. The two lines continued in competition until 1891 when the Castle Line completely abandoned Dartmouth and London for Southampton and future sailings alternated with the Union SSCo's steamers. For the next decade all homeward-bound Castle Line mailboats called at Plymouth to land passengers, mail and specie. Up to three Castle Line steamers per month were calling and included: the *Grantully Castle, Northam Castle, Tantallon Castle, Harlech Castle, Roslin Castle, Dunnotar Castle* and the *Drummond Castle*.

The British & Colonial Steam Navigation Co. Ltd. was formed by Bucknall Brothers in 1891. Four years later the company entered the passenger trade to South Africa. Three ships were ordered, each carrying 66 passengers. On 20 June 1895 the Company's steamship

The PERSIC *in Plymouth Sound, photographed from a tender.*
SYDNEY GOODMAN COLLECTION

The KAISER WILHELM DER GROSSE in Plymouth Sound on 18 June 1906. Passengers are transferring to the SMEATON.
BRITISH RAILWAYS

Johannesburg called at Plymouth on the return leg of her maiden voyage. The British & Colonial Steam Navigation Co. Ltd. provided a round Africa service, calling at Madeira, Cape Town, Port Elizabeth, East London, Port Natal, Delagoa Bay, Zanzibar, Bombay, Aden, Suez, Port Said and Algiers. At the time of the *Johannesburg*'s arrival, the company's other two steamers, the *Fort Salisbury* and the *Bulawayo*, were making their maiden voyages. The distinctive funnel markings of the fleet, a ring of white diamonds on a black ground – known as Bucknalls' teeth – became a regular monthly feature in Plymouth Sound. The service, which soon after terminated at the Cape, was the forerunner of Ellerman's east African and South African services which were calling at Plymouth in the 1950s.

During the 1890s the Pacific Steam Navigation Company (PSNCo) introduced an eastbound Plymouth call on their fortnightly Liverpool–Valparaiso service. Ships included the *Galicia, Orcana, Orissa, Iberia, Britannia* and *Orpressa*. One voyage by the *Orpressa* in 1895 illustrates both the route and the nature of the Plymouth call. Departing from Valparaiso on 17 April, the *Orpressa* made calls at: Coronel (Chile) on 18 April; Punta Arenas (Chile) 23 April; Montevideo 27 April; Rio de Janeiro 2 May; Bahia (Salvador, Argentina) 5 May; Pernambuco (Brazil) 6 May; St. Vincent 11 May; Lisbon 17 May; La Pallice ? May; Plymouth 20 May; and Liverpool 21 May. At Plymouth 114 mailbags, 14 crates of parcels

and a number of passengers were landed.

While liners of the PSNCo. continued to call during the 1930s and 1950s, the line's Plymouth call, in common with other South American lines, was subject to seasonal and other fluctuations of trade.

As previously noted, HAPAG had maintained a Plymouth call since the late 1860s. The company's use of the port was subject to variations however. In 1889 their express trans-Atlantic steamers resumed a westbound Southampton call, while the frequency of the eastbound Plymouth call was reduced. In 1895 the HAPAG express liners; *Augusta Victoria, Normannia* and *Fürst Bismarck* made some homeward calls at Plymouth and thereafter the call re-gained some importance. In 1899 all of HAPAG's intermediate trans-Atlantic liners were calling at Plymouth, westbound and eastbound.

Norddeutscher Lloyd (NDL) was established in 1856 in Bremen. During the 1870s steamers of the line's South American service called at Plymouth. In 1897 NDL took delivery of a new trans-Atlantic liner – a 14,350 tons gross, four funnelled liner named *Kaiser Wilhelm Der Grosse*. She was built by the Vulkan Yard of Stettin to be the largest and fastest ship in the world. If she failed to complete her maiden voyage at her specified speed NDL reserved the right to refuse delivery. She left Bremen on 19 September 1897, calling at Southampton on the 20th. She completed the Atlantic crossing from the Needles to the

Ambrose Light in 5 days, 22 hours and 30 minutes, at an average speed of 21.39 knots – the fastest maiden voyage ever. Her homeward run, timed between the Ambrose Light and the Eddystone, was completed in 5 days, 15 hours, 25 minutes, at an average speed of 21.87 knots. The *Kaiser Wilhelm der Grosse* then made her first Plymouth call. Her maiden voyages set new records for the Channel route. On her third homeward voyage the *Kaiser Wilhelm der Grosse* achieved an average of 22.35 knots, making her the fastest ship in the world. Other NDL express liners calling at Plymouth eastbound in 1897 included the *Havel, Saale, Trave* and *Lahn*. In the first half of 1899 NDL established a weekly express service between Bremen–Southampton–New York, with eastbound calls at Plymouth.

THE LONDON & SOUTH WESTERN RAILWAY AND OCEAN QUAY

The Union SSCo's mail ships resumed a homebound Plymouth call in 1893, but it was the L&SWR's Ocean Quay in Devonport which provided the disembarkation facilities. The L&SWR's interest in the liner trade lay in their involvement with the development of Southampton Docks. Southampton became the principal competitor for the liner trade, mostly at the expense of Liverpool. The gradual shift of trans-Atlantic passenger lines from Liverpool to Southampton and the Channel ports worked to Plymouth's advantage – being suitably positioned as an early port-of-call for all of northern Europe's trans-Atlantic liners.

L&SWR trains first ran into the Three Towns (Plymouth, Devonport and Stonehouse) on 18 May 1876, terminating at their newly built Devonport Station. A short, goods only branch was opened, linking quays on the Devonport shore of Stonehouse Pool to the L&SWR mainline at Devonport Station. The quays and the branch were built under the authority of the Stonehouse Pool Improvement Act. When the Union SSCo. at Southampton, announced its intention to reinstate a Plymouth call, the L&SWR determined to win the passenger business itself. The railway company entered into an agreement with the Stonehouse Pool Improvement Company to lease premises and quays at Richmond Walk in Stonehouse

Pool. Waiting rooms and Customs examination rooms were built and the development was named Ocean Quay. The L&SWR chartered a local passenger steamer, the 104 tons gross, steel paddler *Princess Royal*, of the Saltash, Three Towns & District Steamboat Co. Ltd., to attend liner calls.

The first liner worked by the L&SWR at Plymouth was the Union Line's *Athenian*. She was sighted off the Lizard at noon on Sunday 29 October 1893. At 2pm she was signalled from Rame Head and the *Princess Royal* steamed out to meet her in Plymouth Sound. The L&SWR could only offer to disembark passengers as they had no authority to land mail at Ocean Quay. The *Princess Royal* was therefore joined by the GWR's *Sir Richard Grenville*, which took off the mails.

Aboard the L&SWR tender were: G. T. White, Superintendent of the L&SWR; Mr Vallance, Divisional Superintendent at Exeter; and other officials. Not to be outdone the *Sir Richard Grenville* carried a contingent of GWR officials, including: James Rooney, Superintendent of the Great Western Docks; H. Quigley, Assistant Divisional Superintendent of the GWR; and Mr A. Ward, the representative for H. J. Waring & Co, Shipping Agents. The mails were transferred to the GWR tender and conveyed to the Great Western Docks where they were put on the night mail train to London. The L&SWR party meanwhile faced some embarrassment, as only 11 passengers disembarked, each for destinations served by the GWR between Penzance and Bristol – none for the L&SWR's special London train that was waiting at Devonport. Apparently a larger number would have landed but nobody had been informed of the new Plymouth call at Cape Town. The L&SWR's problems were not helped by the Union SSCo.'s refusal to pay their passengers' rail fares to London – as was the case with the Castle Line and the GWR. Furthermore the L&SWR charged passengers for landing by tender at Plymouth, while the GWR had long since adopted a system of invoicing the relevant shipping agent, thereby transferring the matter of reimbursement to the shipping company's discretion. The rather dejected party of L&SWR officials returned to

Richmond Walk and inspected their new facilities. Once the teething troubles were sorted the L&SWR catered for large numbers of the Union SSCo's passengers.

Calls by both the Union SSCo. and the Castle Line ended in 1900 when the two companies amalgamated as the Union-Castle Mail Steamship Co. Ltd. In future a monthly call was maintained by Union-Castle's intermediate service only.

LINER CALLS FOR MAY & JUNE 1895

———————— MAY ————————

DATE	LINER	LINE	FROM
1	ATRATO	RMSPCo.	W. INDIES
1	OCEANIC	WHITE STAR	HONG KONG
4	RUAPEHU	NZSCo.	LONDON
4	CUZCO	ORIENT	LONDON
5	PESHWAR	P&O	CALCUTTA
5	TONGARIRO	NZSCo.	N. ZEALAND
5	PARRAMATTA	P&O	SYDNEY
6	PENINSULAR	P&O	BOMBAY
6	GRANTULLY CASTLE	CASTLE	CAPE TOWN
7	OPHIR	ORIENT	AUSTRALIA
9	HIMALAYA	P&O	BOMBAY
10	SCOT	UNION SSCo.	CAPE TOWN
12	LUSITANIA	ORIENT	(CRUISE)
13	GOLCONDA	BI	CALCUTTA
15	MEDWAY	RMSPCo.	S. AMERICA
15	MERKARA	QUEENSLAND R. M.	AUSTRALIA
17	OCEANA	P&O	SYDNEY
18	TANUI	NZSCo.	N. ZEALAND
18	OPHIR	ORIENT	LONDON
18	IONIC	SS&A	LONDON
19	NORHAM CASTLE	CASTLE	CAPE TOWN
20	OROPESA	PSNCo.	VALPARAISO
20	NUBIA	P&O	CALCUTTA
21	LAGOS	BRITISH & AFRICAN	W. AFRICA
21	ORIZABA	P&O	AUSTRALIA
23	CALEDONIA	P&O	BOMBAY
24	NORMAN	UNION SSCo.	CAPE TOWN
28	GARONNE	ORIENT	(CRUISE)
29	ORINOCO	RMSPCo.	S. AMERICA
29	RENA	BI	CALCUTTA
30	AUSTRALIA	P&O	AUSTRALIA
30	RUAHINE	NZSCo.	N. ZEALAND
31	TANTALLON CASTLE	CASTLE	CAPE TOWN
31	SHANNON	P&O	CALCUTTA

———————— JUNE ————————

DATE	LINER	LINE	FROM
1	LUSITANIA	ORIENT	LONDON
3	TONGARIRO	NZSCo.	LONDON
6	GALICIA	PSNCo.	VALPARAISO
8	ORIENT	ORIENT	AUSTRALIA
9	HARLECH CASTLE	CASTLE	CAPE TOWN
10	GANGES	P&O	BOMBAY
10	GOTHIC	SS&A	N. ZEALAND
11	DUNERA	BI	CALCUTTA
11	ATHENIAN	UNION SSCo.	CAPE TOWN
12	DON	RMSP	S. AMERICA
15	ROSLIN CASTLE	CASTLE	CAPE TOWN
15	ORIZABA	ORIENT	LONDON
16	MASSILIA	P&O	AUSTRALIA
17	DUKE OF ARGYLL	QUEENSLAND R. M.	AUSTRALIA
17	ORCANA	PSNCo.	VALPARAISO
18	BENGAL	P&O	CALCUTTA
20	LIGURIA	ORIENT	AUSTRALIA
20	JOHANNESBURG	BRITISH & COLONIAL	AFRICA
22	MOOR	UNION SSCo.	CAPE TOWN
23	CARTHAGE	P&O	BOMBAY
26	PARA	RMSP	S. AMERICA
28	DUNNOTAR CASTLE	CASTLE	CAPE TOWN
28	VICTORIA	P&O	AUSTRALIA
29	RUAHINE	NZSCo.	LONDON
29	ORIENT	ORIENT	LONDON
30	KAIKOURA	NZSCo.	N. ZEALAND

Notes: 1 May – OCEANIC had been running between San Francisco and China/Japan for Occidental & Oriental Line. She was returning to UK for general overhaul. 7 May – OPHIR with England cricket team aboard, returning from test series in Australia. 12 May – LUSITANIA returning from pleasure cruise to Constantinople. 28 May – GARONNE returning from 40 days cruise in the Mediterannean.

Notes: 3 June – TONGARIRO was delayed at Plymouth due to boiler trouble. Repairs were made by Willoughby's in Millbay and she eventually sailed on 14 July.

CHAPTER THREE

THE CHANNEL ROUTE

1900 – 1919

IMPROVEMENTS AT MILLBAY

A number of improvements at Millbay, initially proposed in 1898, were gradually completed during the early 1900s. A new entrance to the Inner Basin, with hydraulically controlled gates, was opened on 1 November 1902. The re-alignment and repositioning of the lock gates facilitated the lengthening of Millbay and Trinity piers. Trinity Pier was also widened and new warehousing was erected. The planned extension of Millbay Pier gained urgency in 1903 when the City of Cork Steam Packet Company's *Lee* collided with the pier on 9 November, damaging about 40 feet at the seaward end. The Princess Royal Pier pontoon was provided with an awning and the pontoon bridge was moved to the southern side of the pier proper, spanning directly from the pier's short stone abutment. Passengers for the GWR's French and other steamer services could thus embark from the pontoon landing, leaving the actual pier free for the use of tenders.

In 1908 a scheme was proposed to develop Wembury Bay, just around the eastern headland of Plymouth Sound, as an ocean liner terminal port. A Bill was promoted; the Wembury (Plymouth) Commercial Docks and Railway Bill 1909. It was planned to create a harbour by the erection of breakwaters and to build the necessary wharves and piers for the docking of lin-

The SMEATON at Millbay Pier c. 1905. Note the new awning on the pier and the alterations to the SMEATON's bridge – compared to the earlier photograph on page 22. On East Quay is one of the GWR's bullion vans, No. 820.
BRITISH RAILWAYS

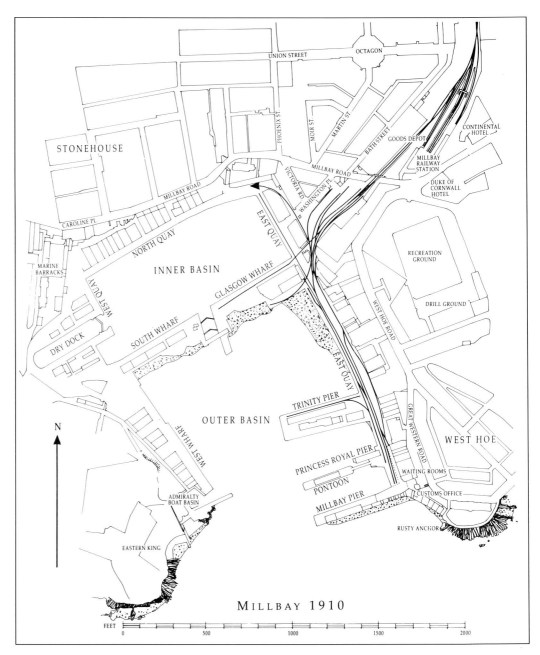

MILLBAY 1910

The ex-Mersey ferry paddle steamer CHESHIRE, at Plymouth c. 1906.

DOUGLASS HOPPINS COLLECTION

ers. It was also proposed to build a railway from the harbour to join the line of the Plymouth & Dartmoor Railway at Plymstock – over which both the GWR and L&SWR had gained running rights. The measure was opposed by the GWR amongst others and it did not obtain Parliamentary sanction.

The steel paddle steamer *Cheshire* was purchased by the GWR in 1905 to serve as a tender at Millbay. Originally built in 1889 as a Mersey ferry for Birkenhead Town Council, the *Cheshire* measured 137.2 x 28.0 x 11.4 feet, 387 tons gross.

THE GWR'S RESERVE WEYMOUTH STEAMERS AT PLYMOUTH

On 1 October 1899 the GWR and L&SWR amalgamated their steamer services to the Channel Islands and some GWR passenger steamers, namely the *Lynx*, *Antelope* and *Gazelle*, became redundant. In 1900 the *Gazelle* was sent to Plymouth. Her forward lifeboats were removed to leave a clear landing stage for liner passengers. She was used as a tender and excursion vessel at Plymouth until 1907. During this time she was also used as a standby vessel at Weymouth. In 1907 she was converted to a cargo vessel and until 1912 used at Plymouth and Weymouth on the GWR's Nantes and Brest cargo services.

The *Antelope* and the *Lynx* were sent to Plymouth in 1903, to offer assistance in attending liners. The *Lynx* had already spent some time at Plymouth during 1901 and until 1907 she worked as a tender and excursion vessel there. She was also used at Weymouth and Jersey during this period. After 1907 she was used on the French services, being converted to a cargo ship in 1912. The *Antelope* worked as a tender and excursion ship at Plymouth 1903–1906. In 1907 she ferried personnel to the White Star liner *Suevic*, which was stranded off the Lizard. In the same year she ran an

excursion to Brest. Subsequently both the *Antelope* and *Lynx* were chartered by French growers to carry their strawberries to Plymouth. Following the arrival of two new, purpose built tenders in 1908, alternative work was sought for the Lynx class steamers.

TRANS-ATLANTIC LINES

The turn of the century heralded an upturn in the volume of liner traffic using Plymouth as a port-of-call. Numbers rose from 444 liner calls and 12,919 passengers in 1901, to 546 liner calls and 21,181 passengers five years later. The Channel Route, which best served

The GAZELLE at Plymouth c.1900 on tendering duty. Her forward lifeboats have been removed from their position aft of the bridge and two gangways can be seen on the boat deck. She flies the NDL houseflag from her foremast – the line that has chartered her.
DOUGLASS HOPPINS COLLECTION

The LYNX at Millbay, at the start either of a coastal excursion or a French trip.
A. KITTRIDGE COLLECTION

S. S. "Deutschland" at Plymouth.

HAPAG's trans-Atlantic record breaker, the DEUTSCHLAND, at Plymouth.
A. KITTRIDGE COLLECTION

The CHESHIRE receiving mails from the DEUTSCHLAND. One of the mail bags reads 'New Zealand via San Francisco'. Pacific mails were transported across America by rail and embarked aboard mailships on the east coast.
A. KITTRIDGE COLLECTION

the whole of Europe, became more popular with trans-Atlantic passengers and Plymouth's share of the traffic increased as a result.

In 1900 only HAPAG and NDL amongst the trans-Atlantic lines were maintaining a regular Plymouth call. In that year HAPAG took delivery of their 16,500 tons gross, four funnelled liner, the *Deutschland*. She was built to beat the *Kaiser Wilhelm der Grosse* and become the fastest ship in the world. On 4 July 1900 the *Deutschland* departed from Hamburg, calling at

Plymouth on 6 July *en-route* to New York. She made the crossing between the Eddystone and Sandy Hook in 5 days 15 hours 46 minutes, at an average 22.42 knots – a new record. She departed from her Hoboken berth on 18 July, making the return voyage – Sandy Hook to Eddystone – in 5 days 14 hours 6 minutes at an average of 22.46 knots, the fastest ever crossing. The *Deutschland* claimed the 'Blue Riband of the North Atlantic' and triumphantly called into Plymouth to land mail and 100 passengers before continuing to Cherbourg and Hamburg.

In 1902 HAPAG's Hamburg–Channel Ports–New York mail service was maintained by the liners *Moltke* and *Blütcher*, both of which called at Plymouth – the *Moltke* having called on her maiden voyage in June 1902. In 1904 Dover was substituted as the British port of call for all HAPAG steamers. Fortunately for Plymouth, Dover proved unsuitable and HAPAG resumed Plymouth calls in August 1906. Since 1905 the company's express service to New York was maintained by the *Deutschland*, the *Amerika* and the *Kaiserin Auguste Victoria*. The mail service was maintained by the *Pennsylvania*, *Pretoria*, *Patricia* and the *Graf Waldersee*. When two new steamers; the *President Lincoln* and the *President Grant* (so named to appeal both to emigrants to the United States and American passengers) entered service in 1907, Southampton was substituted as the westbound British port of call.

Amongst HAPAG's other lines was a service the to Gulf of Mexico. Liners on this route included the *Westerwald*, *Fürst Bismarck* (1905) and *Corcovado*, all of which called in at Plymouth.

NDL took delivery of their second four funnelled express liner, the *Kronprinz Wilhelm*, in 1901. She was fitted with wireless telegraph equipment (as was the *Kaiser Wilhelm der Grosse* after successful experimentation in the previous year). The *Kronprinz Wilhelm* called in at Plymouth on her maiden eastbound voyage. In the following year the liner claimed the westbound record with a crossing of 5 days 11 hours 57 minutes. Two new four funnelled liners, the *Kaiser Wilhelm II* and the *Kronprinzessin Cecilie*, joined the NDL fleet

RECEIVING MAILS H.A LINER DEUTSCHLAND AT PLY

in 1903 and 1907 respectively. The *Kaiser Wilhelm II* gained the 'Blue Riband', holding the westbound record from 1904 and the eastbound record from June 1906, until October 1907 when Cunard's new four stacker, the *Lusitania*, broke all previous records. In addition to their four funnelled express liners, ships of NDL's intermediate trans-Atlantic service also made calls. These liners included the *Bremen* (1897), *Grosser Kürfurst*, *George Washington* (at 25,570 tons gross, the company's largest liner to date), and the *Prinz Freidrich Wilhelm*.

The Inman liners *City of New York* and *City of Paris* were absorbed into the American Line in 1893 and their names were shortened to

NDL's intermediate trans-Atlantic liner, the GROSSER KÜRFURST, in Cawsand Bay. Evening calls by German trans-Atlantic liners offered a welcome bonus for the villagers of Cawsand and Kingsand, in the form of the latest waltzes being played by the ships' orchestras. Some residents of the Rame Peninsula strolled to Cawsand Bay for the purpose of watching the liners and listening to the music.
SYDNEY GOODMAN COLLECTION

The American Line's NEW YORK calling at Plymouth on 15 July 1903.
SYDNEY GOODMAN COLLECTION

New York and *Paris*. In 1895 the *St Louis* and *St Paul*, the third and fourth largest liners in the world at the time, were launched from the yard of William Cramp & Sons, Philadelphia, for the American Line. The line gained the new U.S. Mails contract which was switched from Philadelphia–Liverpool to the New York–Southampton route. By 1897 the American Line had become one of the foremost lines in the trans-Atlantic passenger trade carrying more first and second class passengers to New York than any other. In 1903 the American Line's *St Louis*, *St Paul*, *New York* and *Philadelphia* (ex-*Paris*) started calling at Plymouth eastbound, *en-route* to Southampton.

RAILWAY RIVALRY AT PLYMOUTH

The American Line's decision to make a Plymouth call before proceeding to Cherbourg and Southampton was similar to that taken by the Union SSCo. in 1893. Once again the L&SWR were determined to retain the passenger traffic that they were losing from Southampton. The accommodation at Ocean Quay was improved – waiting friends and relatives of liner passengers were the principal recipients of the hospitality offered by the buffet and waiting rooms. The railway company also brought in its own tender. Built by J. & G. Thomson Ltd. of Clydebank in 1896, the *Victoria* measured 220.5 x 28.15 x 16.3 feet, 709 tons gross. For the L&SWR she had maintained their Jersey–Granville/St Malo services. Her mainmast was removed and the forward lifeboats moved aft, to leave a clear landing deck. She arrived in Plymouth on 25 March 1904.

Meanwhile, since December 1903, the *St Louis* and *St Paul* had commenced calling at Plymouth and the GWR handled both the mail and passenger traffic. But, in April 1904, with improvements completed at Ocean Quay, the *Victoria* on station and Ocean Special trains laid on, the L&SWR gained the passenger trade from the GWR.

The station, waiting rooms and Customs inspection rooms at Ocean Quay were located in an island structure, 350 feet long, with a railway line on either side, so that two L&SWR Ocean Specials could stand at the station simultaneously. The Ocean Specials comprised of trains of eight wheeled corridor carriages and included a dining saloon and sleeping cars (for night time landings). The 56 feet long sleeping cars had seven single and two double berths – complete with brass bedsteads. Having learned from their mistake in 1893, the L&SWR levied no landing charges.

The race to prove which railway could reach London fastest started in the early hours of Saturday 9 April 1904 with the arrival of the *St Louis*. The liner radioed that her arrival time would be four hours earlier than initially expected and personnel had to be summoned to Ocean Quay by telephone and messenger just before midnight to prepare for her arrival.

S S NEW YORK ON OCEAN MAIL SERVICE PLYMOUTH 15.7.03

The ST LOUIS in Plymouth Sound. The houseflag of the American Line (white with a blue eagle) flies from her main mast. Lower down is the U.S. Mails pennant.
SYDNEY GOODMAN COLLECTION

The *Sir Richard Grenville* attended the mails for the GWR. The *Victoria* departed from Ocean Quay at 2am with some passengers bound for Cherbourg. Aboard the L&SWR tender were Henry Holmes – Superintendent of the railway, and Dugald Drummond – Chief Mechanical Engineer of the L&SWR. The *Victoria* came alongside the *St Louis* at 3.25am. At 3.44am, having embarked 57 passengers the *Victoria* returned to Ocean Quay. Customs procedures

Table of railway timings between Plymouth and Waterloo Station, London. From 'Plymouth as an Ocean Port', published by Plymouth Chamber of Commerce.

OCEAN MAILS AND PASSENGERS LANDED AT PLYMOUTH

by the American Line Steamers for the Three months of July, Aug. and Sept., 1906.

DATE. 1906	NAME.	MAILS.	PASSEN-GERS.	Time Liner Anchored.	Transf'g Mails from Liner to Tender	Transf'g Passengers & Baggage from Liner to Tender.	Tender arrived at Quay.	Transf'g Mails from Tender to Train	Mail Train left	Passenger Train left.	Mail Train arrived London.	Passenger Train arrived London.	REMARKS.
					Minutes	Minutes		Minutes					
July 8	St. Louis	982	...	1.2 a.m.	19	...	1.50 a.m.	22	2.13 a.m.	...	6.43 a.m.	...	Mails only.
		...	109	...	...	27	1.56 a.m.	...	...	2.42 a.m.	...	7.25 a.m.	Passengers and Baggage only.
,, 14	Philadelphia	822	...	4.42 a.m.	14	...	5.25 p.m.	20	5.47 p.m.	...	10.49 p.m.	...	Mails only.
		...	94	...	...	19	5.26 p.m.	...	...	5.57 p.m.	...	10.23 p.m.	Passengers and Baggage only.
		...	...	...	...	...	...	...	...	...	...	...	
,, 22	St. Paul	1136	...	1.35 p.m.	22	...	2 26 p.m.	20	2.47 p.m.	...	7.25 p.m.	...	Mails only.
		...	104	...	...	22	2.24 p.m.	...	...	3.10 p.m.	...	7.54 p.m.	Passengers and Baggage only.
		...	...	...	...	...	...	...	...	...	...	...	
Aug. 4	New York	1122	...	12.35 p.m.	18	...	1.10 p.m.	23	1.35 p.m.	...	6.17 p.m.	...	Mails only.
		...	67	...	...	19	1.12 p.m.	...	...	1.35 p.m.	...	6.17 p.m.	Passengers and Baggage only.
		...	...	...	...	...	...	...	...	...	...	...	
,, 11	St. Louis	822	...	9.55 a.m.	17	...	10.37 a.m.	19	10.58 a.m.	...	3.15 p.m.	...	Mails only.
		...	99	...	...	24	10.39 a.m.	...	...	11.10 a.m.	...	4.8 p.m.	Passengers and Baggage only.
		...	...	...	...	...	...	...	...	...	...	...	
,, 18	Philadelphia	961	...	5.3 a.m.	18	...	5.49 a.m.	21	6.12 a.m.	...	10.27 a.m.	...	Mails only.
		...	41	...	...	20	5.44 a.m.	...	...	6.5 a.m.	...	10.48 a.m.	Passengers and Baggage only.
		...	...	...	...	...	...	...	...	...	...	...	
,, 25	St. Paul	958	...	4.31 p.m.	16	...	5.6 p.m.	21	5.29 p.m.	...	9.33 p.m.	...	Mails only.
		...	33	...	...	20	5.13 p.m.	...	...	5.26 p.m.	...	10.8 p.m.	Passengers and Baggage only.
Sept. 1	New York	1074	...	8.40 a.m.	20	...	9.42 a.m.	25	10.8 a.m.	...	2 16 p.m.	...	Mails only.
		...	63	...	...	25	9.33 a.m.	...	...	9.57 a.m.	...	2.37 p.m.	Passengers and Baggage only.
,, 8	St. Louis	783	...	1.35 a.m.	19	...	2.31 a.m.	23	2.55 a.m.	...	7.7 a.m.	...	Mails only
		...	27	...	...	24	2.24 a.m.	...	...	2.48 a.m.	...	7.39 a.m.	Passengers and Baggage only.
,, 15	Philadelphia	1079	...	9.51 a.m.	16	...	10.27 a.m.	21	10.50 a.m.	...	3.10 p.m.	...	Mails only.
		...	52	...	...	14	10.25 a.m.	...	...	10.48 a.m.	...	3.33 p.m.	Passengers and Baggage only.
		...	...	...	...	...	...	...	...	...	...	...	
,, 22	St. Paul	907	...	5.10 p.m.	16	...	5.51 p.m.	19	6.11 p.m.	...	10.23 p.m.	...	Mails only.
		...	21	...	...	20	5.53 p.m.	...	...	6.4 p.m.	...	10.44 p.m.	Passengers and Baggage only.
		...	...	...	...	...	...	...	...	...	...	...	
,, 29	New York	1117	...	12.12 p.m.	17	...	12 49 p.m.	24	1.15 p.m.	...	5.28 p.m.	...	Mails only.
		...	39	...	...	17	12 46 p.m.	...	...	1.4 p.m.	...	6.8 p.m.	Passengers and Baggage only.

Top left: The Waiting Room at Ocean Quay.
DOUGLASS HOPPINS COLLECTION

Top right: The Refreshment Room at Ocean Quay. A sign above the counter reads 'DINNER PROVIDED ON THE TRAIN'.
DOUGLASS HOPPINS COLLECTION

Above: The two baggage inspection rooms at Ocean Quay. Porters trucks are variously lettered 'Stonehouse Pool' or 'Devonport'. The letter boards overhead could be run along the bar from which they are hung and were used to sort baggage according to the initial letters of the owners.
DOUGLASS HOPPINS COLLECTION

were completed and the four coach Ocean Special departed at 5.03am. The train reached London's Waterloo Station at 9.36am, 19 minutes after the GWR mail train arrived at Paddington.

In the afternoon of 23 April 1904 the *St Paul* arrived in Cawsand Bay. The mail and passenger trains departed from their respective quays simultaneously at 3.51pm. Timed between Millbay Crossing (GWR) and Devonport Station (L&SWR) at 3.55pm and 4.1pm respectively, the GWR Ocean Mail train arrived at Paddington at 8.7pm – four minutes

after the L&SWR Ocean Special had arrived at Waterloo. When the *Philadelphia* called on 30 April 1904 the GWR regained the record with a time of 3 hours 54 minutes and an average speed 63.24 mph., against the L&SWR time 4 hours and average speed 57.50 mph.

The GWR were steadily building up the speeds, preparing for publicity coup that would trump the L&SWR decisively. The *Kronprinz Wilhelm* arrived at Plymouth on 9 May 1904. Passengers and 1,085 mailbags were taken off by the GWR tender. The Ocean Mail train was headed by the locomotive *City of Truro*. Also

The Cremyll Ferry approaching Admirals Hard c. 1907. In the background is Ocean Quay with a passenger train drawn up at the station. Moored at the quay is the ATALANTA.
A. KITTRIDGE COLLECTION

The VICTORIA off Cremyll at the mouth of the River Tamar.
A KITTRIDGE COLLECTION

aboard the train was Charles Rous-Martin, a railway performance and speed recorder. The *City of Truro*'s objective was to head the first train in the world to travel at 100 mph. This was achieved when the train was claimed to have reached 102.3 mph on the Wellington Bank. The end sorting coach was detached at Bristol and the engine *Duke of Connaught* replaced the *City of Truro*. The final time for the journey was 3 hours 54 minutes at an average 63.26 mph.

Both of the railway companies speeded up the work undertaken by the tenders and Customs. When the *New York* arrived on 16 September 1905 at 8.57 am., the tender *Victoria* was alongside within seven minutes. She departed from the liner at 9.11am, arriving at Ocean Quay 21 minutes later. The Ocean Special departed at 9.53 am, just 56 minutes after the *New York*'s arrival.

The 'spirited' competition between the two railway companies was revealed in its true light on 1 July 1906, the day the GWR opened their faster Castle Cary route to Paddington. The liner *New York* arrived at Plymouth and the L&SWR determined to spare no effort in the race to London. Forty three passengers from the *New York* boarded the Ocean Special at Ocean Quay. At 1.57am the express derailed at Salisbury Station while attempting to negotiate a 30 mph left hand curve at over 70 mph. Twenty four passengers were killed. It was not unusual for the L&SWR's Ocean Specials to race through Salisbury at speed, but, in the opinion of O. S. Nock, in his book, *The London & South Western Railway*, a change of engine

class, which altered the centre of gravity of the motive power, had tipped the scales to disaster. The wreckless racing stopped forthwith. Passengers from the very next American Line

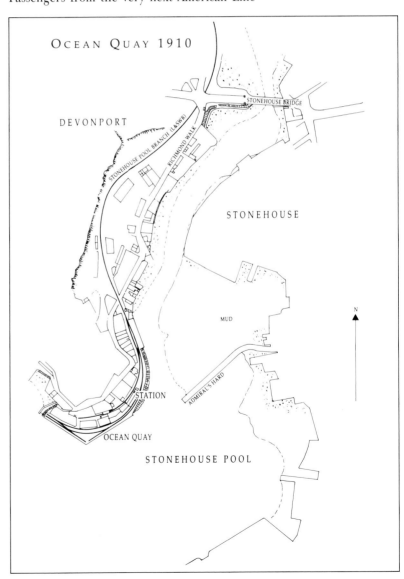

The L&SWR's tender ATALANTA.
WORLD SHIP SOCIETY

The general arrangement diagrams of the SIR FRANCIS DRAKE and the SIR WALTER RALEIGH of 1908.
NATIONAL MARITIME MUSEUM

experienced an even gentler journey to Waterloo of 5 hours 2 minutes.

The dangerous races to London had ended but the L&SWR had no intention of giving up their liner trade at Plymouth. In 1907 a purpose built passenger tender was launched from the yard of Gourlay Bros. & Co. (Dundee) Ltd. She was named the *Atalanta* and measured 170.3 x 32.2 x 15.3 feet., 577 tons gross. The *Victoria* returned to Jersey but relieved the *Atalanta* during the winter.

TENDERS

Two new tenders, the *Sir Francis Drake* and the *Sir Walter Raleigh*, were delivered to the GWR in 1908. They were identical twins and joined the fleet of four tenders already in service: the *Smeaton*, *Sir Richard Grenville*, *Cheshire* and the paddle steamer *Sir Francis Drake* – the latter vessel being laid up in reserve and renamed *Helper*. The new *Sir Francis Drake* was launched on 18 February 1908. Trials were undertaken on 6 April. The two new tenders were designed by C. T. Ramsay, the GWR's Consulting Naval Architect and Engineer. They

arrival, the *St Louis*, on 8 July 1906, encountered train times of 4 hours 30 minutes by the L&SWR to Waterloo and 5 hours 33 minutes by the GWR Ocean Mail to Paddington. Passengers from the *Philadelphia*, which was the following American Line arrival on 14 July,

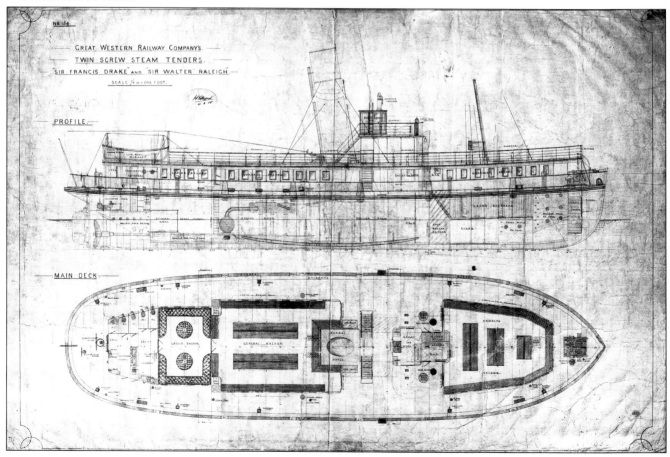

The SIR FRANCIS DRAKE at Fishguard in 1909. Astern is one of the Fishguard-Rosslare steamers .

BRITISH RAILWAYS

were built by Cammell, Laird & Co. Ltd. of Birkenhead. The twin screw, steel, steamers measured: 145.8 x 38.6 x 14.1 feet, 478 tons pied the middle with a ladies' saloon astern. A promenade deck extended from bow to stern, over the deckhouse and out to the sides of the

Above: The General Saloon aboard the 'DRAKE or 'RALEIGH of 1908.
Right: The Ladies Saloon aboard the 'DRAKE or 'RALEIGH.
A. KITTRIDGE COLLECTION

The SIR WALTER RALEIGH prior to her maiden voyage as a tender at Millbay in 1908. Note the baggage railway in the foreground and the stowage vans

upon stanchions. Accommodation for officers and crew was provided forward on the lower deck. Lighting throughout was electric. Each tender had Board of Trade certificates to carry 590 passengers within the smooth water limits of Plymouth Sound, and 400 passengers between Exmouth and the Lizard and between Barmouth and Tenby – the tenders had been designed with service at

designed to emit their fumes above the passenger decks of the liners they were attending. In August 1909 the *Sir Francis Drake*, along with the *Smeaton*, was transferred to attend Cunard's liners at Fishguard. The *Sir Walter Raleigh* also spent some time at Fishguard in 1909.

THE INTERNATIONAL MERCANTILE MARINE COMPANY

or associated with the International Mercantile Marine Company (IMM), a company formed by the American financier J. P. Morgan in 1902, with the object to gain control of trans-Atlantic passenger shipping. Within a year of its formation the IMM controlled the International Navigation Co. – which owned the American Line and its Belgian flagged associate Red Star Line, the Atlantic Transport Line, the Dominion Line, the Leyland Line (already owned by Morgan) and, to the consternation of the British, Morgan's company bought the White Star Line. The IMM also concluded an operating alliance with NDL and HAPAG. Harland & Wolff, the British shipbuilders, allied itself to the new syndicate and also acquired controlling interest in NASM. IMM then turned its attentions to Cunard in a bid to complete the 'Morganisation' of the trans-Atlantic passenger trade. To prevent IMM achieving its virtual monopoly, the British Government, faced with a loss of influence over a substantial part of its passenger carrying merchant fleet, were pressed into agreeing a loan to Cunard of £2,600,000 repayable in 20 years at a rate of 2.75% p.a. The money was provided for the construction of two new express trans-Atlantic liners, namely the *Lusitania* and the *Mauretania*. In return Cunard agreed not to sell out to IMM.

CUNARD AT FISHGUARD

Remaining independent of IMM, Cunard in 1908 was the only major trans-Atlantic passenger line still wholly committed to the Liverpool–New York route. The *Lusitania* entered service on 7 September 1907 and in October gained the 'Blue Riband' from the *Kaiser Wilhelm II* with a westbound journey of 4 days 19 hours 52 minutes and an average 23.99 knots. Her eastbound record breaking time was 4 days 22 hours 53 minutes at an average 23.61 knots. It must be noted that the timings were for the voyage between Ambrose Light (New York) and Queenstown (Cobh) in Ireland – the 'Blue Riband' record was based on average speed, not just elapsed time.

The *Mauretania* made her maiden voyage on 16 November 1907. Cunard evidently felt they were losing business to IMM and the Channel Route and in August 1909 they started eastbound calls at Fishguard – to land mails and offer London and Continental bound passengers the opportunity of avoiding Liverpool and reaching London earlier.

The SMEATON alongside the MAURETANIA at Fishguard on 30 August 1909, taking off the mails.

BRIAN JACKSON COLLECTION

The SIR FRANCIS DRAKE departs from the MAURETANIA at Fishguard on 30 August 1909.

BRIAN JACKSON COLLECTION

The Fishguard & Rosslare Railways & Harbours Company – a joint venture company of the GWR and the Great Southern & Western Railway of Ireland – undertook a massive dock development at Fishguard, aimed at gaining Irish steamer and railway traffic from the London & North Western Railway at Holyhead. The opportunity also presented itself to win some of the London & North Western Railway's liner traffic from Liverpool by inviting Cunard to make a call before proceeding to Liverpool.

The *Mauretania* made the line's first call at Fishguard on 30 August 1909. Three tenders were available: the *Smeaton* was transferred from Plymouth to attend the mail; the new *Sir Francis Drake* was also transferred from Plymouth to cater for the passengers; and a third tender, the *Great Western* from the GWR's Waterford service, took off the passengers' baggage. The *Mauretania* dropped anchor at Fishguard at 1.20pm on 30 August. She landed 897 mailbags and 240 passengers. The passengers reached London at 7.28pm.

Special 'Cunard Ocean Express' trains were laid on for the visits of both the *Mauretania* and the *Lusitania*. In 1910 14,000 passengers and 55,000 mail bags were landed at Fishguard. Cunard's express trans-Atlantic liners increased the frequency of their calls but the Fishguard call never fulfilled the GWR's expectations. After the First World War Cunard finally switched its New York service to Southampton and the GWR picked up calls both from Cunard's New York and Canadian services at Plymouth.

OCEAN QUAY CLOSURE

On 13 May 1910 the L&SWR and GWR signed an Agreement covering railway related items in the Westcountry, a revision of the pool-

The LUSITANIA at Fishguard in 1909, viewed from the Fishguard–Waterford steamer, the GREAT WESTERN (of 1902), which served as a tender at Fishguard. One of her lifeboats has been removed to make space for baggage.

BRIAN JACKSON COLLECTION

ing agreement concerning Channel Islands services and a zoning of French services. Included in the Agreement was the transfer of all L&SWR liner tender services at Ocean Quay to the GWR. The GWR agreed to purchase the *Atalanta* and she returned to Southampton before leaving to take up station at Fishguard on 13 June. Her arrival in west Wales released the *Sir Francis Drake* and *Smeaton* to return to Plymouth. Ocean Quay Station closed in the following year. The L&SWR continued to use the Stonehouse Pool Branch for goods only and the rail link survived until 1964.

The return of the *Sir Francis Drake* and the *Smeaton* rendered the *Helper* truly redundant and in August 1910 she was sold to Joseph Constant, Shipbroker, who in turn sold her in the following year to Cosens & Co., Ltd., of Weymouth, for use as a passenger steamer. At Weymouth the *Helper* ran public excursions to Lulworth Cove and helped fulfil Cosens' contract for providing liberty boat services between Portland naval base and Weymouth.

The *Cheshire* was sold for breaking in 1912 to W. Ritsher of Hamburg.

MORE TRANS-ATLANTIC LINES

NASM returned to Plymouth on 7 August 1910 when their 24,000 tons gross liner, the *Rotterdam*, made an eastbound call *en-route* between New York, Boulogne and Rotterdam. By the following month the *Rotterdam* and her fleet sister, the *Nieuw Amsterdam*, had established a fortnightly eastbound call at Plymouth.

The White Star Line announced its intention to run their express trans-Atlantic service from Southampton to New York via Cherbourg in 1907. The liners *Teutonic*, *Majestic*, *Oceanic* and *Adriatic* were transferred from Liverpool to maintain the new route. In 1910 White Star's Southampton–New York liners maintained a weekly Plymouth eastbound call, before proceeding to Cherbourg and Southampton. The company planned to replace the four liner service with three new super-liners and in October 1910 the *Olympic* was launched from Harland & Wolff's yard in Belfast. On the stocks beside her was taking shape her sister ship the *Titanic*. The third ship would be the *Britannic*. Each ship exceeded 45,000 tons

gross – the largest ships in the world. The *Olympic* made her maiden voyage from Southampton on 14 June 1911, calling at Cherbourg–Queenstown (Cobh)–New York westbound, and New York–Plymouth–Cherbourg–Southampton eastbound. The *Olympic* replaced both the *Teutonic* and the *Adriatic* on the Channel Route. When the *Majestic* was also withdrawn at the end of

NASM's ROTTERDAM in Cawsand Bay with the SIR FRANCIS DRAKE or SIR WALTER RALEIGH of 1908 alongside.
A. KITTRIDGE COLLECTION

Right: The OLYMPIC in Cawsand Bay c. 1911/12.
SYDNEY GOODMAN COLLECTION

Below: The OLYMPIC in Cawsand Bay photographed from a tender. Ahead the SIR FRANCIS DRAKE or SIR WALTER RALEIGH flies the White Star Line's houseflag (red burgee with white five pointed star) and a Royal Mail pennant.
SYDNEY GOODMAN COLLECTION

1911, ships of the American Line supplemented the service until the *Titanic* entered service on 10 April 1912. It was planned that the three ships: *Olympic*, *Titanic* and *Oceanic* would maintain the weekly service. In the Smoking Room aboard the *Titanic* there hung a Norman Wilkinson painting 'Approach to Plymouth Harbour'. At Harland & Wolff's yard construction of the third giant liner had commenced. The catastrophe which befell the *Titanic* on the night of 14/15 April is well known – it is estimated that 1,502 people lost their lives in the worst peacetime shipping disaster at sea.

The *Olympic* was *en-route* to Plymouth when her radio room received the news. All entertainments ceased forthwith. She had passed Sandy Hook on Saturday 13 April and was expected at Plymouth on the following Friday to land 300 passengers, 1,808 mailbags and 459 bars of silver. A wireless message was received by Weekes, Phillips & Co. on the Friday, from Capt. Haddock of the *Olympic*, stating that he was 394 miles off the Lizard at 8.30am, and expected to arrive at Plymouth at 4.30am on the following day. Her passage had been delayed due to her offer of assistance to the rescue ships and *Titanic* survivors if required.

At 8.06am on 28 April the Red Star liner *Lapland* dropped anchor in Cawsand Bay. Disembarking were 162 passengers, 1,610 mailbags, £250,000 specie and 167 survivors of the crew of the *Titanic*. Some 20–30 journalists and large crowds awaited ashore to see the survivors. The dock had been closed to all journalists and others without a pass. At the gates of Millbay Pier local borough constables assisted the dock police in keeping control. The survivors embarked aboard the *Sir Richard Grenville* which was the first tender to leave the *Lapland*. However, she did not head for Millbay but cruised around the Sound until the *'Drake* and *'Raleigh* had left the liner. The *'Grenville* remained out in the Sound as the *Lapland* was cleared for departure to Cherbourg. The object, it appeared, was to allow the passengers and mails to be landed first. All was not as it seemed however and the *Western Morning News* 29 April 1912 reported:

That would have been a reasonable arrangement and one which could not be found fault with were the general arrangements for the reception and detention of the crew less open to question. But there is another possible explanation to the delay in bringing the *'Grenville* to the dockside. Each man was to be served with a Board of Trade subpoena to give evidence before the Receiver of Wrecks at Plymouth and it must have taken some time to convince the crew that it was out of regard for their personal convenience that they would be detained at the Great Western Docks until the Receiver of Wrecks had taken their depositions. Some of the men have wives and families at Southampton and elsewhere and hoped that on landing they would have sped homeward by the boat express.

It was during this loitering in the Sound that the officers of the Seafarers' Union came into prominence. They had learnt the designs of the Board of Trade and White Star Line and manoeuvring their boat alongside the tender explained the position to the men, who thereupon made it known that they would refuse to give evidence at all unless the restriction placed upon their liberty was removed and they were taken home in the evening by special train.

The demand was conceded and after two hours in the Sound the *'Grenville* steamed into Millbay. The continued interference by the White Star Line seems all the more hypocritical when it is appreciated that the surviving crew – men and women – were considered discharged from the time the *Titanic* had sunk, and from that time on had been wholly dependent upon generous American charity.

The Western Morning News concluded that 'The whole procedure which the officials sought to enforce is inexplicable and were only modified following the demands made on the men's behalf by the Seafarer's Union'.

By the afternoon, with 167 depositions completed, the male survivors were allowed to talk to journalists and visit the town centre if they wished. They departed by train in the evening. Almost 24 hours after landing in Britain, and 15 days after the disaster, the surviving crew members arrived back at Southampton to be re-united with their families.

COLONIAL & OTHER LINES
By 1910 over 40% of the annual total of line calls at Plymouth were trans-Atlantic liners. In

1895 P&O and the Orient Line we
biggest customers, but by 1910 the
surpassed by HAPAG, NDL, White S
American Line. The colonial line
not in decline – there were an est
liner calls in 1895 and the increase
annual calls in 1910 is accounted fo
the increase of trans-Atlantic line ca
liners remained vitally important to
liner trade representing just under
pre-First World War total.

THE CARIBBEAN

Since 1901 Elder Dempster'
Direct West India Mail Steamship C
between the West Indies and A
Ships of the line were each na
Jamaican ports and locations: *Por*
Antonio, *Port Maria*, *Port Moran*
Kingston. They had white hulls and
goes of fruit, primarily bananas. T
Direct service was subsidised by a
mail contract, the mail being
Plymouth. When the mail contra
1910, so too did the Imperial Direct

AFRICA

In 1900 the Union SSCo. and
Line amalgamated as the Union-
Steamship Co. Ltd. Most Plymou

Company, following that company's
from the joint venture. In May
e her maiden voyage to Australia,
undertook a cruise for invited
n London to Plymouth, anchoring
d overnight.

erdeen Line remained alone in
an outward bound call only. Their
London (Royal Albert Dock),
Tenerife, Cape Town, Melbourne
, with mails being carried between
nd Australia. A monthly call was
with the steamers; *Damascus* (with-
3), *Moravian*, *Salamis* (withdrawn
ocles* (withdrawn 1906), *Miltiades*,
nd *Pericles* (from 1908). Two new
over 11,000 tons entered service in
se were the *Themistocles* and

ar's Australian liners were still call-
lymouth. On 17 March 1907 the
homeward bound from Australia
ssengers. Many retired to bed early
on for the morning's disembarka-
nouth. At 10.30pm, in driving rain
he *Suevic* struck rocks on the
Reef off the Lizard. The bow sec-
ship was firmly aground, but she
king. The Falmouth and Lizard

Coverack lifeboats. In six hours over 600 passengers and crew were safely rescued, not one person was lost. The rescue remains as the largest number of lives saved by the Royal National Lifeboat Institute in one incident. The decision was taken by the salvage company to blast away the bow section of the liner, which was stuck on the rocks. Blasting started on 26 March and continued until the remainder of of the ship floated free on 2 April. It was planned to beach the liner at Plymouth and carry out temporary repairs, but as the threat of bad weather abated she was towed to Southampton instead. On 5 October Harland & Wolff launched a new bow section which was fitted to the ship in Southampton on 4 November. On 18 January 1908 the *Suevic* once again returned the White Star's Australian service.

A few hours after the *Suevic* had gone aground on 17 March, the African Steamship Company's *Jebba* – also *en-route* to Plymouth and suffering from the same weather conditions – went aground on the South Devon coast (see above).

P&O maintained a fortnightly service to Australia with the liners: *Macedonia, China, Mongolia, Marmora, Morea, Mooltan, India, Maliva* and the *Moldavia*. The *Medina* and *Maloja* joined the service in 1911. Each ship called in at Plymouth on their homeward voyage. There was also a P&O branch line service to Sydney via the Cape.

Both the SS&A/White Star Joint Service liners and the NZSCo's ships continued to run from London to New Zealand with a Plymouth call in each direction. SS&A/White Star's liners included the *Arawa, Tanui, Ionic* and *Athenic*.

NZSCo. vessels called twice monthly (home/out) and included: the *Ruapehu, Rimutaka, Rotorua, Turakina, Tongariro* and *Ruahine*.

INDIA & THE EAST

P&O's service from Bombay called homeward bound *en-route* to London at 10 to12 day intervals. Liners calling in 1910 were: the *Egypt, Arabia, Persia, Oceana, Himalaya, Matuna, Delhi* and *Marmora*. In 1914 the *Kaisar-I-Hind* entered service on the the Bombay mail route. She was the only ship of

The Aberdeen Line's MILTIADES in Plymouth Sound.
SYDNEY GOODMAN COLLECTION

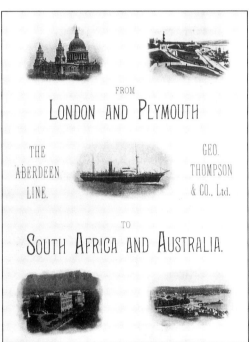

The Aberdeen Line brochure of 1909. With the MILTIADES and Plymouth Hoe included amongst the illustrations on the cover.
A. KITTRIDGE COLLECTION

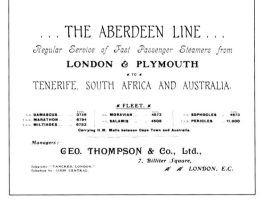

From the Aberdeen Line brochure 1909.
A. KITTRIDGE COLLECTION

The Aberdeen Line's THEMISTOCLES or DEMOSTHENES in Plymouth Sound in 1911/12, with the CHESHIRE alongside.
A. KITTRIDGE COLLECTION

her class and set a new Bombay–Plymouth record of 17 days 20 hours 52 days.

BI steamers from Calcutta called at Plymouth *en-route* to London and included the *Jelunga, Matiana, Mombasa* and *Golconda*.

P. Henderson & Company ran to Burma with their British & Burmese Steam Navigation Co. Ltd. Popularly known as Paddy Henderson's, the line's *Amarapoora* and *Irrawaddy* called at Plymouth occasionally. On 7 December 1910 the *Irrawaddy* landed passengers in Plymouth Sound and then proceeded to Devonport Dockyard to unload a cargo of teak for the Admiralty. Henderson ships called at Plymouth until the Second World War and in the 1930s included the *Chindwin* and *Martaban.*

CANADA

The Allan Line, long associated with the Canadian passenger trade, started calling westbound at Plymouth in 1912, *en-route* between London–Quebec–Montreal. The *Sicilian* made the company's first call, followed by the *Corinthian*. Other liners on the route were the *Scotian* and *Ionian*. The call did not survive the First World War.

SOUTH AMERICA

The Booth Line had maintained a service between Liverpool and the River Amazon since the 1860s, the Booth family having extensive interests in the rubber trade. In 1910 their passenger ships included the *Anthony, Lanfranc, Hilary* and the new *Hilderbrand* of 1910. The

The CORINTHIC of the White Star Line's Australia service, in Plymouth Sound.
SYDNEY GOODMAN COLLECTION

CHAPTER FOUR

TRANS-ATLANTIC TOURISTS & OCEAN TRAVELLERS

1920 – 1944

DOCK DEVELOPMENTS AND NEW TENDERS

Attending an ever decreasing number of wartime calls, the *Sir Richard Grenville* had remained on station at Millbay throughout the First World War. She was rejoined in January 1919 by the *Sir Francis Drake* and the *Sir Walter Raleigh*, and later still by the *Atalanta*, as they were released from Admiralty service. The *Smeaton* remained a while longer at Brest, embarking US troops. Surplus to immediate requirements the *Sir Richard Grenville*, *Atalanta* and the *Smeaton* were laid up, although the *Sir Richard Grenville* was certificated and periodically pressed into service with a made up crew. Both the *Smeaton* and the *Sir Richard Grenville* were unsuccessfully advertised for sale at the Baltic & Mercantile Exchange on 29 November 1921. The *Atalanta* remained laid up at Millbay until she was sold to the Royal Mail Steam Packet Company on 3 May 1923. Her departure signalled a reprieve for the *Smeaton* and *Sir Richard Grenville* and, following refits, they resumed service on a more regular basis.

Under the terms of of the Railways Act 1921 the Great Western Railway absorbed the major South Wales railway companies, along with their respective docks at Swansea, Port Talbot, Barry, Cardiff and Newport. By the time the grouping was completed in 1923 Millbay Docks had become a constituent of one of the world's largest dock systems and a period of constructional improvement followed.

The dry dock was modernised in 1925 and North Quay was improved and provided with three new electric cranes. In 1927 an electric conveyor was installed on East Quay for handling Ocean Mails. The outer basin of Millbay Docks consisted of a 35 acre area. A 19 feet

draft was available at Millbay Pier at low water. West Wharf was 800 feet long and offered 28 feet draft at low water. By 1938 the largest ship that had ever entered Millbay was the 13,000

Advertisement from the Shipping World Year Book 1938.

COURTESY NIGEL COOMBES

The SIR RICHARD GRENVILLE as she appeared after the First World War.
DOUGLASS HOPPINS COLLECTION

The SIR FRANCIS DRAKE with the SIR WALTER RALEIGH (forward) berthed at Millbay Pier and the SMEATON with the SIR RICHARD GRENVILLE (forward) berthed at the Princess Royal Pier pontoon. Photograph c. 1925.
A. KITTRIDGE COLLECTION

ton *Kenilworth Castle* – subsequent to her collision with HMS *Rival* in 1918.

Between 1921 and 1928 the annual liner calls at Plymouth doubled from 350 to 708. It was decided therefore to replace the ageing *Smeaton* and *Sir Richard Grenville* with two new tenders, each to be nearly twice the size of the 'Drake and 'Raleigh. The first was ordered from Earle's Shipbuilding & Engineering Co. Ltd., of Hull and launched on 14 May 1929. She was named *Sir John Hawkins* and measured 930 tons gross, 172.5 x 43.1 x 14.6 feet. Two sets of triple

expansion engines were made by her builders. She carried 800 passengers on her class three certificate. Trials were undertaken on 4 July 1929 and the *Sir John Hawkins* arrived at Plymouth four days later.

The Ulster Steam Tender Company had a contract for attending liners of the Canadian Pacific, White Star, Cunard and Anchor lines when they called into the Belfast Lough. In 1929 the Ulster company was looking for an additional tender to join their steamer, the *Robina*. On 5 September 1929 they bought the *Smeaton* and nine days later she made her first tendering run on the Belfast Lough.

For the second new tender estimates were invited for diesel electric drive, but steam reciprocating machinery was eventually ordered owing to the higher initial cost of the alternative. The new tender was ordered from Earle's Shipbuilding & Engineering Co. Ltd. in 1930, being the last vessel built by that company. Launched on 18 June 1931 she was named *Sir Richard Grenville*. Two sets of triple expansion engines were again supplied by her builders. The boilers however were oil fired on a forced draught system, thus the *Sir Richard Grenville*'s funnel was elliptical and shorter than that of the coal fired *Sir John Hawkins*. The full speed of the *Sir Richard Grenville* was 13 knots and accommodation was provided for over 800 pas-

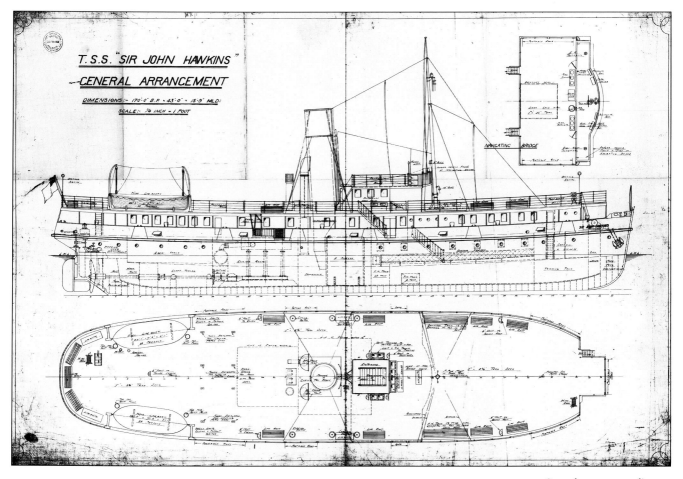

General arrangement diagram for the SIR JOHN HAWKINS.
NATIONAL MARITIME MUSEUM

The SIR JOHN HAWKINS *flying the houseflag of the GWR. She is pictured off Staddon Heights having just arrived in Plymouth Sound for the first time on 8 July 1929.*
DOUGLASS HOPPINS COLLECTION

The Dining Saloon of the SIR JOHN HAWKINS. The tables have been set out specially for the photograph, while the upholstered bench seats remain protectively covered. Dinner was only served while the tender was on excursions. A buffet bar system sufficed for liner passengers on the short trip to Millbay.
ASSOCIATED BRITISH PORTS
COLLECTION
SOUTHAMPTON CITY MUSEUMS

Above right: The SIR JOHN HAWKINS' General Saloon with one of a number of writing desks provided for liner passengers.
ASSOCIATED BRITISH PORTS
COLLECTION
SOUTHAMPTON CITY MUSEUMS

sengers and 13 crew. Special attention was paid to the fitting out of the tenders' saloons, to provide warmth and comfort for passengers disembarking from liners during the winter – sometimes in the early hours of the morning. A dining saloon on the lower deck seated sixty four persons and was provided primarily for excursion passengers. The general saloon, smoke room and ladies' lounge were located on the main deck. The promenade deck aboard both new tenders was kept as clear as possible for landing passengers and mail. The after part of this deck was strengthened to receive automobiles from the liners. The *Sir Richard Grenville* measured 896 tons gross, 172.5 x 42.7 x 14.7 feet.

Following the arrival of the new *Sir Richard Grenville* her old namesake was renamed the *Penlee* – the name of the headland in Cawsand Bay which is the western extreme of Plymouth Sound. The *Penlee* was sold to the Dover Harbour Board in 1932 and renamed the *Lady Savile*. At Dover the *Lady Savile* was used as a tender and an excursion steamer.

The tender fleet at Plymouth now comprised of the four steamers which, owing in part to their nomenclature, are perhaps the best remembered: the *Sir Francis Drake, Sir Walter Raleigh, Sir John Hawkins* and the *Sir Richard Grenville*. No further tenders were built or acquired by the GWR and units of the 1932 fleet continued tendering at Plymouth until one by one they were withdrawn from service as the liner trade declined after the Second World War.

Left to right: the SIR RICHARD GRENVILLE (of 1891), SIR JOHN HAWKINS and SIR WALTER RALEIGH at Millbay in 1929. On East Quay are Post Office stowage vans with passenger coaches behind. The small cranes on Millbay Pier could lift off baskets of parcels or mail, and heavier items of baggage.
ASSOCIATED BRITISH PORTS
COLLECTION
SOUTHAMPTON CITY MUSEUMS

The SIR RICHARD GRENVILLE arriving at Plymouth in August 1931. She is pictured outside the Breakwater, making for the western entrance. She was virtually a sister ship to the SIR JOHN HAWKINS but differed in that she was oil fired on a forced draught system. Her funnel was therefore shorter.
The warship moored inside the Breakwater is the Devonport built, Iron Duke class battleship HMS MARLBOROUGH.
ASSOCIATED BRITISH PORTS, MILLBAY

Above left: The Smoke Room of the new SIR RICHARD GRENVILLE in 1931.
ASSOCIATED BRITISH PORTS, MILLBAY

Above: The General Saloon of the SIR RICHARD GRENVILLE, August 1931.
ASSOCIATED BRITISH PORTS, MILLBAY

The Sir Francis Drake and Sir Richard Grenville at Princess Royal Pier pontoon.
DOUGLASS HOPPINS COLLECTION

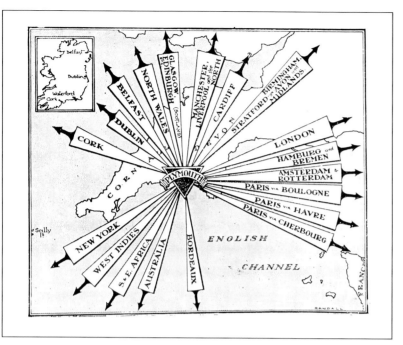

From the publicity brochure 'Plymouth as a Port-of-Call'.
COURTESY DOUGLASS HOPPINS

'England via Plymouth' from a publicity brochure of the 1930s.
COURTESY DOUGLASS HOPPINS

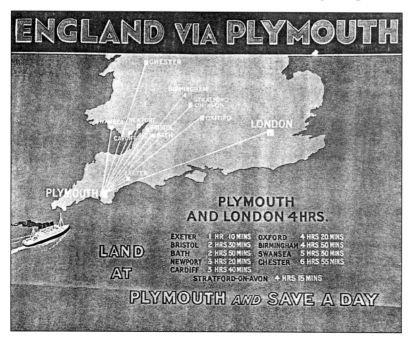

LINE CALLS

It is not surprising that the number of line calls at Plymouth leapt from just 70 during the last year of the war to a total of 263 in 1919. By 1922 however even this figure doubled to 527 liner calls, with 23,000 passengers and 300,000 mailbags being handled. The figures continued to climb towards the all time peak of 788 liner calls in 1930, comprising of 106 outward bound ships (a figure matched only twice before – in 1903 and 1906) and a record 682 homeward bound calls. A total of 41,130 passengers and 307,912 mailbags passed through Millbay in 1930. During this busy period in the history of the liner trade at Plymouth, some 14 shipping companies established new calls. They joined over a dozen other lines that re-established their pre war calls.

TRANS-ATLANTIC LINES

The Emergency Quota Act of 1921 was introduced by the United States government after the war to reduce the number of immigrants entering the country. However, it was from the north Atlantic lines that the greatest increase in Plymouth's post war liner trade came. This apparent contradiction arose with a fundamental change in nature of the trans-Atlantic trade. Sparked in part by Americans' heightened awareness of Europe since the war and fuelled by excess passenger capacity aboard liners due to the US immigration controls, millions of Americans gained the motive and the means to make the pilgrimage back to the 'old country', or to do the 'grand tour' of Europe. It has been estimated that Americans comprised 80% of the post war passenger traffic on the north Atlantic. Landing in Britain or France many travelled through Europe, making their way down to Genoa for the return trip. Steerage accommodation vanished and segregated first, second and third class designations gradually decreased, especially aboard the less class prejudiced American ships. Liners were built or converted to new class designations: cabin class – a combination of 1st/2nd which dispensed with segregation; tourist class – a 2nd/3rd combination; or cabin/tourist – which retained some on-board demarcation. There were also some tourist/third ships which offered economic passage in dormitory accommodation. Lines catered increasingly for the predominantly American trans-Atlantic tourist trade. Plymouth was conveniently placed to take advantage of this change by offering an efficient port-of-call for visitors to Britain before the liners proceeded to the Continent with the balance of the passengers.

NASM profited greatly from Holland's neutrality during the war and in 1917 bought themselves out of Harland & Wolff/IMM control to become independent once again. Their immediate post war voyages continued the

wartime Falmouth call but this was soon substituted by Plymouth. Line calls were made by the company's ships: *Rotterdam, Volendam, Ryndam, Veendam* and the *Nieuw Amsterdam* (of 1906). Later, in 1929, the 30,000 ton, three funnelled *Statendam* entered service. A decade later the 36,000 ton *Nieuw Amsterdam* was completed. On her return maiden voyage the *Nieuw Amsterdam* arrived at Plymouth at 2.40pm on 27 May 1938. Three tenders steamed out from Millbay to greet her, the third tender carrying official visitors, including the Deputy Lord Mayor of Plymouth, the King's Harbourmaster and the Dutch Consul. The *Nieuw Amsterdam* landed 319 passengers and 700 mailbags. She was cleared by Bellamy & Co., shipping agents, and departed at 4.50 pm bound for Boulogne and Rotterdam. In 1939 the sister ships, *Noordam* and *Zaandam* entered service as one class ships, both called at Plymouth.

GERMAN LINES

The huge fleets of both NDL and HAPAG were claimed by the allies as war reparations and many ex-German ships reappeared on trans-Atlantic services in the livery of British and American companies.

The United States Mail Steamship Co. Inc. (USMSCo) arranged to charter ex-German tonnage from the U.S. Shipping Board and provide a service between New York and Bremen – filling the gap left by the absence of NDL. The USMSCo. appointed NDL as their central European agents and agreed to the German company employing their own ships on the route in exchange for the use of their Bremerhaven dock facilities. In June 1921 the 22,000 ton ex-HAPAG liner *Amerika*, renamed the *America*, commenced running from New York to Plymouth, Cherbourg and Bremen. She was joined by the ex-NDL liner *George Washington* in August 1921. The USMSCo. crashed financially later in the same month and all the services were taken over by the U.S. Shipping Board, trading as the United States Lines.

NDL was re-admitted to the North Atlantic

NASM resumed homebound Plymouth calls after the war. In 1929 the line took delivery of the 30,000 ton STATENDAM, *built by Harland & Wolff. She is pictured at Plymouth on 4 May 1929, with the '*DRAKE *or* 'RALEIGH *attending.*
ASSOCIATED BRITISH PORTS
COLLECTION
SOUTHAMPTON CITY MUSEUMS

NGL
NORTH GERMAN LLOYD

Regular Service to
Plymouth · Cherbourg · Bremen
by the
S.S. COLUMBUS
S.S. STUTTGART
S.S. MUENCHEN

to Bremen Direct
by the
S.S. BREMEN, S.S. SIERRA VENTANA,
S.S. YORCK and S.S. LUETZOW

One of NDL's post war super-liners, the 50,000 ton BREMEN, in Plymouth Sound at 6.30 am on 12 September 1931. The design and decor of the BREMEN and her sister ship, the EUROPA, was strikingly functional compared to their older contemporaries. They featured Art Deco styling – similar to Odeon cinemas of the '30s and '40s. Likewise their lines and outward appearance set new standards for successive generations of liners.

ASSOCIATED BRITISH PORTS COLLECTION
SOUTHAMPTON CITY MUSEUMS

Passenger Conference in 1922. Their trans-Atlantic liner *Columbus* of 1913 was claimed by the Allies as war reparations and passed to the White Star Line who renamed her the *Homeric*. Her sister ship, which had been laid down in 1914 but had remained incomplete throughout the war, escaped the Allies attentions and was now completed by NDL as the *Columbus*. Joined by the *München* (1923) and the *Stuttgart* (1924) the three ships became regular callers at Plymouth (eastbound). The 32,000 ton, two funnelled *Columbus* – until 1929 the largest liner that NDL had ever owned – became a familiar sight in Plymouth Sound, calling regularly until the Second World War.

Such was NDL's success during the '20s that in December 1926 the company ordered two huge trans-Atlantic liners. The 50,000 ton sister ships *Bremen* and *Europa* were built by Weser of Bremen and Blohm & Voss of Hamburg respectively. They were launched on consecutive days, but due to fire damage aboard the *Europa*, the *Bremen* was completed first. In July 1929, on her maiden voyage, the *Bremen* broke Cunard's 20 year domination of north Atlantic record crossings with an average speed of 27.83 knots. The homeward voyage,

between Ambrose Light and the Eddystone was completed in the record time of 4 days, 14 hours, 30 minutes, at an average 27.92 knots. The triumphant liner called in at Plymouth before proceeding to Cherbourg and Bremen.

HAPAG, stripped of its enormous fleet at the end of the war, reached agreement with the American Ship & Commerce Corporation to establish a joint service on the north Atlantic. Trading as United American Lines (UAL) they purchased two ex-HAPAG, three funnelled liners from Royal Holland Lloyd and renamed them the *Resolute* and the *Reliance*. The sister ships started a fortnightly service in April 1922, between New York and Hamburg, calling at Plymouth and Boulogne eastbound. Westbound voyages called at Southampton and Cherbourg. In 1923 the eastbound calls were altered to correspond with the westbound route and the Plymouth call was dropped. This was the last that Plymouth saw of HAPAG's north Atlantic involvement. In future only ships of HAPAG's central America service maintained a homebound call.

UNITED STATES LINES

When the U.S. Shipping Board, trading as United States Lines, took over the USMSCo's services in 1921 the liners *America* and *George Washington* continued as before on their New York–Bremen service, calling at Plymouth and Cherbourg eastbound. In February and March 1922 United States Lines introduced two converted wartime 535 class transport ships on a passenger/cargo service between New York, Plymouth, Cherbourg and Bremen. Initially named the *Peninsula State* and *Lone Star State*, the ships were renamed in May as the *President Pierce* and *President Taft*. Later still in 1922 they were renamed as the *President Roosevelt* and the *President Harding*. In the same year United States Lines introduced another passenger/ cargo service between New York and London, calling at Queenstown, Plymouth and Cherbourg. The ships were 502 class transports and included the *Centennial State*, *Panhandle State*, and the *Old North State*. These were renamed in May as the *President Adams*, *President Monroe* and *President Van Buren*. The three ships were joined later by

two more 502s, the *President Polk* and the *President Garfield* and a weekly service was established. In September 1923 the five 502 class ships were sold to the Dollar Line and the service was taken over by the American Merchant Lines (AML) with five 7,000 ton ex-transports: the *American Merchant, American Banker, American Farmer, American Shipper* and the *American Trader*. Initially only 12 passengers were carried, but later the accommodation was increased to cater for 80 passengers. From 1931 the ships were taken over by United States Lines, but the service still traded as the American Merchant Lines. AML ships continued to call at Plymouth on eastbound voyages until 1939.

Two additional United States Lines ships, the *President Arthur* and the *President Fillmore*, both ex-HAPAG ships, called at Plymouth *enroute* between New York and Bremen in 1923

SAILING LIST NO. 18   JUNE 1st, 1923

SAILING SCHEDULE
Subject to Change

UNITED STATES LINES

General   *Offices*
45 BROADWAY – NEW YORK
New York
Cobh (Queenstown)
Plymouth
Southampton
Cherbourg
London
Bremen
Danzig
Sailing from Hoboken N.J.

A United States Lines sailing schedule of 1923 for sailings from Hoboken, New Jersey (New York Harbour) to Europe. All ships of the line, except the LEVIATHAN, *were making regular eastbound Plymouth calls.*

A. KITTRIDGE COLLECTION

and 1924. Also in 1923 the pride of the United States Lines fleet entered service on the north Atlantic. Heralded as the largest liner in the world – a disputed claim which arose from the different US and British measurement systems – the *Leviathan* ran between New York, Cherbourg and Southampton. She was originally HAPAG's giant three funnelled liner, the *Vaterland*, which had been taken over by the United States in 1917 as a troop ship. Another ex-HAPAG ship, the *President Grant* (of 1903), was renamed the *Republic* and entered service in 1924, making a Plymouth call eastbound. The United States Lines ships: *Republic, America, George Washington, President Roosevelt* and *President Harding* maintained a weekly eastbound call at Plymouth.

The *President Roosevelt* was involved in a dramatic rescue in January 1926. She received a distress call from the British cargo vessel *Antigone*, which was in difficulty after her grain cargo had shifted in the heavy seas. The *President Roosevelt*, commanded by Capt. George Fried, stood by the British ship for four days until all of her crewmen were rescued. Two crewmen from the *President Roosevelt* lost their lives during the rescue. When the American ship eventually reached Plymouth she was welcomed by spectators on the sea front. The officers and crew of the ship were thanked by the Mayor of Plymouth at a public reception and awards were later presented by Lloyds of London.

The United States Lines fleet changed ownership twice and in 1931 was controlled by the IMM. In August 1932 the line's new 20,000 ton cabin class liner *Manhattan* made her maiden voyage, calling at Plymouth eastbound. When her sister ship, the *Washington*, entered service in May 1933 the *Leviathan* was laid up. But the U.S. Shipping Board,

Pictured in Cawsand Bay on 2 May 1932, the LEVIATHAN was the flagship of the United States Lines. Formerly HAPAG's VATERLAND, she passed to the US Shipping Board as war reparations, after serving first as a US troopship during the war. The photograph belies her enormous proportions. The LEVIATHAN was advertised by the United States Lines as the 'World's Greatest Ship'. This disputed claim was later moderated to 'America's Greatest Ship'.

ASSOCIATED BRITISH PORTS
COLLECTION
SOUTHAMPTON CITY MUSEUMS

which still exercised influence over line, insisted that the *Leviathan* return to service. In June 1934 the *Leviathan* made five round trips between New York and Southampton, with a Plymouth call. Her last voyage commenced on 1 September, calling at Plymouth, Havre and Southampton. She arrived back in New York for the last time on 14 September 1934. A heavy loss was made on each of her 1934 voyages and she was withdrawn from service for the last time. The United States Lines ships; *Manhattan, Washington, President Roosevelt* and *President Harding* continued calling at Plymouth until 1939.

Another American line to start eastbound calls after the war was the long established Atlantic Transport Line (ATL). Since 1882 this American owned, British flagged fleet, had run between London and New York. The company was best remembered in the west of England for the wreck of their steamer *Mohegan* on the Manacle Rocks, off St. Keverne in Cornwall in 1898, with the loss of 106 lives. ATL was taken over by IMM in 1902. From 1923 until the company ceased to operate in 1932, ships of the ATL fleet called monthly at Plymouth. They included: the *Minnekahda* – a tourist third liner which re-entered post war service for ATL in 1924; *Minnewaska* – a 22,000 ton passenger/cargo liner built by Harland & Wolff in 1923; and the *Minnetonka* – a sister ship to the *Minnewaska*.

IMM's Red Star Line also called at Plymouth after the war. The company's liners were; the *Zeeland, Lapland, Pennland* (calling initially as the *Pittsburgh*, having been transferred from White Star), *Arabic* (ex-*Berlin* of NDL, which was also transferred from White Star), and Red Star's flagship, the three funnelled, 27,000 ton liner *Belgenland* which called at Plymouth while she was on regular trans-Atlantic service. Red Star ran between New York–Antwerp, with eastbound calls at Plymouth and Cherbourg.

CUNARD

The changing nature of the north Atlantic passenger trade prompted Cunard to announce its intention to move their express trans-Atlantic terminus from Liverpool to Southampton in 1919. Eastbound calls were

The MAURETANIA in Cawsand Bay in 1927, with the SIR WALTER RALEIGH steaming out to attend.
DOUGLASS HOPPINS COLLECTION

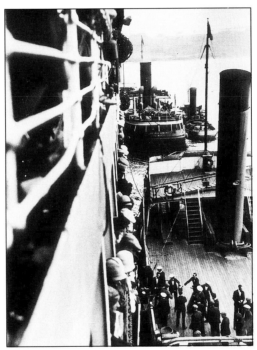

The SIR FRANCIS DRAKE (nearest) and the SIR JOHN HAWKINS alongside the Cunard's flagship, the BERENGARIA.
ASSOCIATED BRITISH PORTS, MILLBAY

made at Plymouth to enable passengers to disembark before a Cherbourg call was made prior to docking in Southampton. Both the *Mauretania* and the company's flagship *Berengaria* called, each landing large numbers of passengers and mails. On 7 April 1925 the *Mauretania* arrived at Plymouth at 5am, having made the crossing between Ambrose Light-Eddystone Light in 5 days 4 hours 9 minutes at an average 25.29 knots. Tenders left Millbay at 5.15am and two hours later had landed 126 passengers and 3,781 mailbags. Meanwhile, the *Mauretania* was cleared for Cherbourg by W. T. Leaman, the Cunard Agent at Plymouth, and she departed at 7am. A special train left Millbay

Cunard's BERENGARIA (ex IMPERATOR) was a near sister ship to the United States Lines' LEVIATHAN. She is pictured in Cawsand Bay with the SIR WALTER RALEIGH departing and the 'HAWKINS, 'DRAKE and two tugs still in attendance. Her first call on 22 July 1930 was made to help passengers make up time lost when the liner experienced propeller trouble on the voyage from New York. Two special trains were laid on at Millbay. The first was a Pullman which took 115 first class passengers to Paddington. The second train carried 23 first class and 220 second class passengers.

The trio of giant, three funnelled liners launched by HAPAG before the First World War was completed by the BISMARCK, which was taken over by the White Star Line in 1922 and renamed the MAJESTIC. She made her first Plymouth call on 4 September 1930.

ASSOCIATED BRITISH PORTS
COLLECTION
SOUTHAMPTON CITY MUSEUMS

Pier at 8.10am, arriving at Paddington at 12.08pm. (officially timed from Millbay Crossing to Paddington in 3 hours 47 minutes). The *Mauretania* landed 262 passengers at Cherbourg in the afternoon and arrived at Southampton at 6.30pm to land a further 238 passengers. The ship's achievement in making all three Channel calls in one day was applauded, but it should be noted that even with these record timings the Plymouth passengers had arrived in London six hours before the liner even docked in Southampton.

Cunard claimed that they never raced across the Atlantic and refused to acknowledge the Blue Riband or to accept the Hales Trophy when it was introduced in the 1930s. However, when the *Bremen* broke the *Mauretania*'s 20 year old trans-Atlantic records in 1929, Cunard's ageing liner suddenly replied within one month with a personal eastbound record of 27.22 knots between Ambrose and the Eddystone (in reply to the *Bremen*'s 27.92 knots). Furthermore, she proceeded from Plymouth to Cherbourg at a startling 29.7 knots.

In February 1934, as a condition for government assistance in the completion of their new super-liner, Cunard agreed to amalgamate with the struggling White Star Line, forming Cunard White Star Ltd. (White Star had been bought out of IMM by the ambitious Royal Mail Group which subsequently crashed financially.) The Cunard super-liner in question was to be the 80,774 ton *Queen Mary*, which entered service in 1936. She made her first Plymouth call on her eastbound maiden voyage, anchoring in Cawsand Bay. She was obscured from sight at Plymouth by a sea mist but the local excursion boats, *City of Plymouth*, *Western Belle* and others made a quick profit by offering trips to view the liner. On 12 April 1938, after an exceptionally stormy crossing, forty of the *Queen Mary*'s passengers required treatment ashore. A fleet of ambulances stood by at Millbay.

Cunard also operated the liners *Andania*, *Antonia*, *Ausonia*, *Aurania*, *Ascania* and *Alaunia* on their London–Southampton– Quebec–Montreal service. Subject to variations in the service, each of these 'A' class liners called at Plymouth on the return journey. During the early months of 1925 the liners are listed in the *Western Morning News* as arriving from New York and Halifax. The change of itinerary was forced in winter months due to ice in the St Lawrence River. A typical winter arrival was the *Antonia*'s on 27 January 1925. She anchored in Plymouth Sound at 11.20am, from New York via Halifax. Out of 165 passengers on board, 51 were landed at Plymouth, plus 455 mail bags. She was cleared By W. T. Leaman at 12.15pm for Cherbourg. 'A' class liners of the Cunard White Star Line continued to call until 1939.

CGT

The Compagnie Générale Transatlantique returned to Plymouth in 1922, when their express liners *Paris* and *France* introduced a call both west and eastbound. Large numbers of mailbags were transferred in each direction. CGT increased their use of Plymouth and by 1925, in addition to the *Paris*, *France* and the *De Grasse* of 1924, on the New York route, liners from the company's Caribbean services were also calling in both directions. These ships included the *Macorris*, *Pellerin de Latouche*, *Flandre* and *Cuba*. In 1931 the 13,000 ton *Colombie* started calling at Plymouth, having been built specially for the West Indies/Antilles service.

In their British advertisements of 1925 CGT claimed:

> Plymouth has repeatedly proved itself the quickest transit port between New York and London. The same applies in the reverse direction. The French Line steamships sail from Plymouth direct to New York.

At about 10.30am on Thursday 18 April 1929 the 34,500 ton CGT liner *Paris* was cautiously approaching Plymouth in a thick fog. She was *en-route* from Le Havre to New York with 624 passengers aboard. A further 40 passengers were due to embark at Plymouth. Having been delayed by the fog all morning, Capt. Yves Thomas radioed Haswell & Co, the CGT agents at Plymouth, that he expected to anchor in Cawsand Bay at 11am. and the *Sir Francis Drake* was dispatched from Millbay. Soon after 10.30am passengers and crew aboard the *Paris* felt a 'sharp jolt' and the liner came to a halt. Off her port bow, now in full view, was the Eddystone Lighthouse. All morning the lighthouse keepers had been firing the

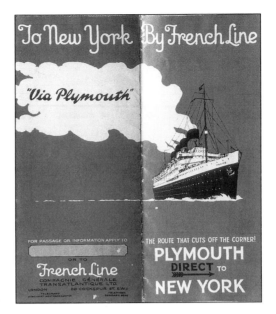

CGT's Plymouth brochure for 1930.

A. KITTRIDGE COLLECTION

fog gun, but so dense was the fog that nobody aboard the *Paris* had seen or heard anything until they were aground on the Eddystone Rocks. Capt. Thomas immediately radioed '… want big tugs to get off rocks and take passengers if necessary'. The radio message caused

The back cover of CGT's Plymouth brochure. The top picture is the FRANCE – which made her last Plymouth call in August 1932 and was withdrawn from service. Below, on the left, is an artists impression of the ILE DE FRANCE leaving Plymouth Sound. On the right is the PARIS, which entered service in 1921. At the bottom on the left is the LAFAYETTE – which made her maiden voyage Havre-Plymouth-New York in May 1930. Finally, on the right, is the DE GRASSE which entered service in 1924.

A. KITTRIDGE COLLECTION

Passengers aboard the 'DRAKE or 'RALEIGH departing from the ILE DE FRANCE in Cawsand Bay.
DOUGLASS HOPPINS COLLECTION

a sensation ashore and the naval Commander-in-Chief at Devonport promptly dispatched the RMAS tugs *Retort* and *Rover* and the duty destroyer HMS *Thanet*. The Looe lifeboat headed out to the Eddystone while the Plymouth lifeboat crew was alerted. The *Sir Francis Drake* meanwhile, lacking wireless, was vainly searching for the liner in the fog in Cawsand Bay. Having decided to return to Millbay the tender

MINIMUM RATES
from
Plymouth *to* New York

			£	s.	d.	
First Class	...	s/s "Ile de France"	55	0	0	(w)
	...	s/s "France"	46	10	0	(w)
	...	s/s "Paris"	52	0	0	(w)
Second Class	...	s/s "Ile de France"	30	5	0	(*) (†)
	...	s/s "France" ...	28	5	0	(*) (†)
	...	s/s "Paris" ...	29	5	0	(*) (†)
Cabin Class	...	m/s "Lafayette" ...	32	15	0	(*) (†)
	...	s/s "De Grasse" ...	31	5	0	(*) (†)
Tourist Third		m/s "Lafayette" ...	22	10	0	(*) (†)
Cabin Class		s/s "De Grasse" ...	21	15	0	(*) (†)

(w) Winter Rates (Summer Rates slightly higher).
(*) All year round.
(†) Return tickets at reduced rates are issued.

From the 1930 CGT brochure.
A. KITTRIDGE COLLECTION

nearly collided with the two RMAS tugs racing out to the *Paris*.

Fortunately there was a flat calm and the French liner had grounded on a rising tide. At 12.30pm, with towlines attached, the *Paris* was safely floated clear of the rocks and she made her own way to Cawsand Bay with all her lifeboats swung out and the Admiralty ships standing by. It was reported that she had been holed fore and aft. The liner awaited instructions from CGT, while the ship's officers vainly tried to keep newspaper reporters away. The Looe lifeboat eventually reached the scene of the grounding in one hour and 45 minutes, a time the crew were pleased with. The pulling lifeboat searched in vain for the liner only to be told by the lighthouse keepers that the *Paris* had indeed been aground but had already been floated off. After landing 164 of her passengers at Plymouth the *Paris* returned to Le Havre for docking. In the same fog a trawler went aground at Jennycliff, and both the PSNCo. liner *Orbita* and P&O's *Maloja* were delayed in arriving at Plymouth.

In June 1927 the 43,000 ton *Ile de France* entered service, her very first call out of Havre being at Plymouth. Possibly the best loved trans-Atlantic liner of all time, the *Ile de France* was a firm favourite at Plymouth. Fortunately her association proved to be a long one as she maintained regular calls at the port until withdrawn in 1957.

The *Ile de France* was due to make one of her scheduled calls on Thursday 17 July 1930. At 12.30pm, while she was off the Lizard, a single engined bi-plane was catapulted off machinery installed over her stern. The crew of three followed the coastline of Cornwall and 35 minutes later dropped a mailbag into Plymouth Sound, within 50 feet of a waiting motorboat. The mailbag was fished out by boathook and handed to the custody of a Post Office official. The aircraft continued on to land in Paris, while the motorboat returned to Millbay and the mailbag was put aboard the first train to London at 2.05pm. Plymouth was the only English port where this dramatic, publicity minded, express mail service was performed. During the late '20s and early '30s there were a series of aeronautical feats and stunts per-

CGT's new motor ship, the
LAFAYETTE, pictured on 18
May 1930 in Plymouth Sound
on her maiden outbound voyage
to New York. The 'HAWKINS
and the 'DRAKE or 'RALEIGH
are attending. In the fore-
ground is the pavilion of the
Promenade Pier.
ASSOCIATED BRITISH PORTS
COLLECTION
SOUTHAMPTON CITY MUSEUMS

formed to publicise the possibilities offered by
the advent of air transport. Some shipping
lines responded by attempting to incorporate
an element of air transport on their voyages.
Unfortunately CGT's well planned mail drop
attracted few spectators on Plymouth Hoe and
just twenty minutes after the special mailbag
had been dispatched to Paddington the *Ile de
France* steamed into the Sound to disembark
150 passengers and a further 2000 mailbags.

Two intermediate ships, the *Lafayette* and
Champlain were completed in 1930 and 1932
respectively. Both were used on the New York
service as cabin/tourist liners. The *Lafayette*
called at Plymouth on her maiden voyage and

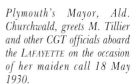

Plymouth's Mayor, Ald.
Churchwald, greets M. Tillier
and other CGT officials aboard
the LAFAYETTE on the occasion
of her maiden call 18 May
1930.
ASSOCIATED BRITISH PORTS
COLLECTION
SOUTHAMPTON CITY MUSEUMS

both liners maintained Plymouth calls.

The fastest, largest, most luxurious liner in
the world, the *Normandie*, entered service for
CGT on 29 May 1935. Following her arrival

A Cyril. H. Gill photograph of
the NORMANDIE entering
Plymouth Sound after her
record breaking crossing in
June 1935. A long blue pen-
nant trails from her masthead.
COURTESY GUY FLEMING

future westbound calls by all CGT ships were made at Southampton instead of Plymouth. The eastbound call remained however and continued until 1961. On her maiden voyage the *Normandie* made Bishop Rock to Ambrose Light in 4 days 3 hours 2 minutes at an average 29.98 knots – a record. Homebound her time was 4 days 3 hours 28 minutes at an average 30.31 knots and she steamed triumphantly into Plymouth Sound, claiming the Blue Riband. She was not a regular caller at Plymouth, an eastbound call on 3 July 1939 was listed as only her second for the season. She made two special westbound calls during the worsening European crisis on the 6th and 27th July 1939, to embark gold bullion, bound for the USA.

The trans-Atlantic passenger trade started to decline in 1930. The number of passengers on the north Atlantic in 1929 had totalled 1,069,000. Six years later the figure had slumped to 460,000. During the same period the number of liners and passengers at Plymouth also declined from 788 calls and 41,130 passengers in 1930 to 596 liners and 34,141 passengers in 1934. The Plymouth statistics do not fully reflect the dramatic decline in the north Atlantic trade, partly because the port was not totally dependent upon trans-Atlantic calls.

CENTRAL AND SOUTH AMERICAN LINES

Plymouth experienced a big increase in trade from lines serving central and South America during the 1930s. In addition to CGT's West Indies services noted above, the Koninklijke West Indische Maildienst (KWIM), also known as Westmail or the Royal West Indies Mailservice, served the Dutch West Indies. After the war KWIM established an outbound and homebound Plymouth call with their liners *Oranje Nassau, Stuyvesant, Crijnssen* and *Van Rensselaer* on their Amsterdam-Paramaribo (Surinam) line. Each ship carried around 70 passengers and were restricted in size to enable them to navigate the Surinam river to Paramaribo. Initially only small numbers of passengers and mail were landed at Plymouth, but the figures increased when KWIM was taken over by the Koninklijke Nederlandsche Stoomboot Maatschappij (KNSM) – the Royal Netherlands Steamship Company – in 1927. The two companies had been in the process of amalgamation since 1910, during which time they maintained their separate identities. Subsequent calls were made under the KNSM houseflag and the above named KWIM ships were joined by the *Venezuela*, the *Cottica*, the twin funnelled 8000

Below: The Hamburg Süd flagship, CAP ARCONA, ran from Hamburg to Buenos Aires. She is pictured on 4 October 1932 entering Plymouth Sound for the first time, with the SIR RICHARD GRENVILLE standing by. The photograph was taken from a Saunders Roe amphibian aeroplane. The pilot was Flight Lieut. T. Rose who was visiting Plymouth with a view to inaugurating an air taxi service from the city.
ASSOCIATED BRITISH PORTS COLLECTION
SOUTHAMPTON CITY MUSEUMS

ton *Simon Bolivar*, the slightly larger *Costa Rica* and the 11,000 ton motorship *Colombia*, all of which ran on KWIM's Colon (Panama) line. KNSM ships were calling up to three times per week, but homebound only. The *Oranje Nassau*, *Stuyvesant*, *Cottica* and *Prins Frederik Hendrik* extended their voyages to New York, returning via Guiana, West Indies, Madeira, Plymouth, Havre and Amsterdam. The numbers of KNSM passengers landing at Plymouth steadily increased, regularly exceeding 100 per call during the 1930s, while mailbags rarely dropped below that figure. In 1938 two new KNSM cargo liners, the *Socrates* and *Pericles*, started calling at Plymouth. Each carried up to 20 passengers on the company's line through the Panama Canal to Chile.

Ships of the Ozean-Dampfer AG (Ozean Line), namely the *Rio Bravo* and *Rio Panuco* of 1924, maintained a service between the Gulf of Mexico and Germany, calling at Hamburg, Southampton, Havana, Tampico and Galveston, with a Plymouth call on their homebound voyage. Named after Mexican rivers the *Rio Bravo* and *Rio Panuco* entered service in 1924 and were twin funnelled liners of 6,000 tons. They had accommodation for 100 passengers and were authorised by the General Postmaster of Germany to fly the Reichspostflagge. The line operated a joint service to the Gulf of Mexico with HAPAG. In 1930 the Ozean Line passed to the ownership of NDL.

The 12,000 ton *Cariba* and *Cordillera* were twin sisters built for HAPAG's West Indies/Central America service. Both ships entered service in 1933 and maintained an eastbound Plymouth call before continuing to Cherbourg, Amsterdam and Hamburg.

Another Hamburg line engaged in the south Atlantic trade was the Hamburg – Südamerikanischen Dampfschiffahrts Gesellschaft, or Hamburg South American Line, better known as Hamburg-Süd. In 1927 their new 27,500 ton liner *Cap Arcona* entered service. She was the largest ship in the south Atlantic trade. The *Cap Arcona* made her first Plymouth call at 3.47pm on Tuesday 4 October 1932, *en-route* from Buenos Aires, Montevideo, Santos, Rio de Janeiro, Lisbon and Vigo, to Boulogne and Hamburg. A party of invited

guests aboard the *Sir Richard Grenville* steamed out to meet the liner. Included in the welcoming party were; Ald. G. P. Dymond (Mayor of Plymouth), A. E. Wonnacott (Chamber of Commerce), D. Laws (Postmaster), J. H. Leatherby (Assistant Postmaster), J. L. Palmer (Editor in Chief of the *Western Morning News*), W. O. Mills (Editor of the *Western Evening Herald*), E. Wyatt Gould (Great Western Docks Manager) and D. G. Hoppins (Chief Clerk at Millbay). They were welcomed aboard the *Cap Arcona* by the Director General of Hamburg-Süd, Theodor Amsinck and Commodore Ernst Rolin, Captain of the liner. 18 passengers and 55 mailbags were landed and the *Cap Arcona* was cleared for Boulogne by Wainwright Bros., agents for the line at Plymouth. The next call was scheduled for 13 November and it was planned that the *Cap Arcona* would call regularly on her homebound voyages.

The Harrison Line (Thos. & Jas. Harrison Ltd of Liverpool) maintained shipping services worldwide. In 1921 a London-West Indies passenger service was started, calling at Antigua, St Kitts, Barbados, Grenada, Trinidad and British Guiana. In the 1930s an eastbound Plymouth call was established by the company's West Indies cargo liners *Ingoma* and *Inanda* and from 1937 the new 6,600 ton *Inkosi*. Small numbers of passengers and mailbags were landed at Plymouth and Fox & Co. cleared the liners for London's West India Docks.

Since 1927 the liners, *Orduna*, *Orbita* and *Oropesa* of the Pacific Steam Navigation Company (PSNCo.) called at Plymouth seasonally on their eastbound voyages from Valparaiso to Liverpool, via the Panama Canal. In 1931 PSNCo. took delivery of their new 17,700 ton liner, the *Reina del Pacifico*. She was

The Harrison Line's INANDA.
A. KITTRIDGE COLLECTION

A striking picture of the PSNCo's 18,000 ton motor ship, the REINA DEL PACIFICO in Plymouth Sound on 8 June 1931. The Royal Mail pennant flies from her yard. The REINA DEL PACIFICO entered service just two months previously – the welcoming flags aboard the tender indicate this is the liner's maiden return voyage.

ASSOCIATED BRITISH PORTS
COLLECTION
SOUTHAMPTON CITY MUSEUMS

a motor vessel, built by Harland & Wolff and had accommodation for 888 passengers. Substantial numbers were landed from the PSNCo. ships – on 3 June 1938 the *Reina del Pacifico* disembarked 252 passengers and 151 mailbags. Her visit two months later was the PSNCo.'s last for the season – the Plymouth call being resumed in the following March.

The black funnelled ships of the Booth Line were still calling occasionally on the eastbound voyages from Manaos to Liverpool. The *Hilary* entered service for the company in 1931. She carried 80 first class passengers and 250 in third class. The third class accommodation was provided primarily for Portugese emigrant workers, travelling to Brazil (Booth Line ships called at Porto and Lisbon). The first class accommodation was popular with passengers making the round trip and the company's pub-

licity slogan – 'A thousand miles up the Amazon' – was coined to promote the line voyages as cruises.

Cruises were also offered by the Lamport & Holt liners *Voltaire* and *Vandyck* which re-entered service in 1932, having been laid up for two years. Both liners continued to offer cruises until 1939, making occasional Plymouth calls.

Five liners were ordered by the Blue Star Line Ltd in 1925 for their South American passenger service. The ships were initially named the *Almeda, Andalucia, Avila, Avelona* and *Arandora*. As some confusion was experienced with similarly named 'A' class liners of the Royal Mail Steam Packet Co., each name was given a Star suffix, which brought them in line with the company's previous nomenclature. The liners were 12,800 ton steamers

An evocative photograph of the Booth Line's HILARY in Plymouth Sound. On their line – Liverpool to Manaos ('A thousand miles up the Amazon') – the black funnelled passenger ships of the Booth Line maintained seasonal Plymouth calls.
ASSOCIATED BRITISH PORTS
COLLECTION
SOUTHAMPTON CITY MUSEUMS

with accommodation for 162 to 180 first class passengers. The *Arandora Star* was refitted as a cruise ship in 1929, but the four remaining liners operated on the Buenos Aires service calling at: Montevideo, Santos, Rio de Janeiro, Tenerife, Madeira, Lisbon, Plymouth, Boulogne and London. In 1931 the *Avelona Star* was converted to a cargo ship. Weekes Phillips were the Blue Star Line's Plymouth agents and a monthly call was maintained.

Pictured at Plymouth on 27 August 1934, whilst engaged on cruise voyages, is the 13,200 ton, Lamport & Holt liner VANDYCK. Both the VANDYCK and her fleet sister, the VOLTAIRE, were built to maintain Lamport & Holt's service from New York to the Caribbean and South America. They were laid up during the late 1920s but in 1932 started a successful career offering cruises from Southampton and Liverpool to Scandinavia, the Mediterranean, Atlantic Isles, West Africa and the West Indies. An occasional call was made at Plymouth.
ASSOCIATED BRITISH PORTS, MILLBAY

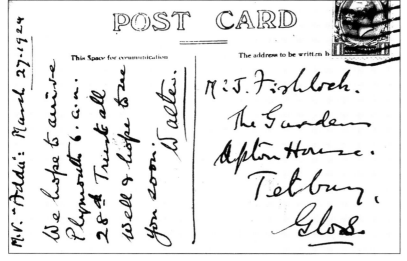

The African Steamship Company's ADDA, depicted on one of the line's postcards. The reverse is dated 27 March 1924 and reads: 'We hope to arrive Plymouth 6am 28th. Trust all well & hope to see you soon'. Posted on arrival at Plymouth, the card will have been delivered later in the day.

ASSOCIATED BRITISH PORTS
COLLECTION
SOUTHAMPTON CITY MUSEUMS

COLONIAL LINES – AFRICA

At the end of the war the world wide interests of the British Empire still remained dependent upon the merchant navy to maintain its lines of communication. The colonial lines, which continued to provide reduced services throughout the war, built up trade quickly when peace returned. Serving Africa was the Union-Castle Line, of which the *Grantully Castle, Llanstephan Castle, Durham Castle, Guildford Castle* and *Garth Castle* were calling at Plymouth outward and homeward bound on east Africa and round Africa services.

Elder Dempster Lines' ships calling in the '20s included the *Adda, Aba, Appam, Abinsi, Abosso, Zaria* and *Ekari*. They operated between Liverpool-Lagos, with some voyages extending to Douala in Cameroon. The *Aba*'s arrival at Plymouth on 17 January 1925 provides an

example of Elder Dempster Lines' Plymouth calls. She had departed from Lagos on 2 January and called at Accra, Sekondi, Sierra Leone and Las Palmas. Delayed by fog off Ushant, the liner eventually landed 84 passengers, 182 mailbags and gold specie at Plymouth. She was cleared for Liverpool where a further 35 passengers and 231 mailbags were bound.

In the late 1920s Elder Dempster introduced two new 9,000 ton motor ships, the *Accra* and the *Apapa*. Both liners catered primarily for first class passengers. In 1935 the 11,000 ton company flagship *Abosso* (2) entered service. The liners called at Calabar, Lagos, Accra, Takoradi, Monrovia, Freetown, Bathurst, Las Palmas, Madeira and Plymouth, terminating at Liverpool. The numbers landing at Plymouth had increased by the late 30s. The *Apapa* on 7 May 1938 landed 220 passengers, 277 mailbags and gold at Plymouth. She was cleared by Travellers Ltd. for Liverpool where just 76 remaining passengers were landed – a further example of Plymouth's significance as a convenient disembarkation port.

The ships of P&O still numbered amongst the most regular of Plymouth's visitors. The list of their calls reads like a 'Who's Who' of famous ships. Amongst the P&O liners from Bombay was the *Kaisar-I-Hind*. She remained on the India Mail for 19 years and in 1925 beat her own Gibraltar–Plymouth record, her new time being 2 days, 13 hours. She remained a popular ship until the end when she was broken up in 1938. The direct service to Bombay was fading out in the mid '30s, the calls being undertaken by ships on the Australian service. P&O's Australian liners included the *Mooltan* and the three funnelled liners, *Naldera* and *Narkunda*, which were built specifically for the route and entered service in 1920. Between 1931 and 1938 the famous 'Straths' entered service: the *Strathnaver* (1931), *Strathaird* (1932), *Strathmore* (1935), *Stratheden* (1937) and the *Strathallan* (1938). Each liner measured over 22,500 tons and carried over 1,000 passengers. Liners on P&O's Far East service from Japan (Yokohama) and China (Shanghai) included the *Ranchi* and the *Rawalpindi*.

BI also continued their Plymouth calls from

Bombay and Karachi. From Calcutta BI ships called at Madras, Colombo, Aden, and Tangier. Ships on this line included the *Mashobra, Merkara, Malda* and *Dumana*. From Beira in Portugese East Africa (now Mozambique), BI's east African service liners called at Dar-es-Salaam, Zanzibar, Port Said, Marseilles, Plymouth and London. Ships on the east African service included the *Modasa, Matiana* and *Mulbera*.

INDIA AND THE FAR EAST

Two Ellerman Lines calling at Plymouth between the wars were; the Ellerman Hall Line from Burma, India and South Africa, and the Ellerman City Line from Karachi and Bombay. Hall Line ships included the *City of Manchester, City of London* and *City of Hong Kong*. City Line ships included the *City of Canterbury, City of Venice* and the *City of Benares*.

The Bibby Steamship Co. Ltd., (Bibby Line Ltd. from 1931), was well known for its troopships and also maintained a fortnightly passenger/cargo service from Liverpool to Colombo and Rangoon. The company's troopships operated from Southampton, mainly to Bombay. When not in use they were laid up on the River Dart in South Devon. Homeward bound from Rangoon, Bibby's passenger liners called at Plymouth during the '30s. The liners included the *Cheshire, Yorkshire, Derbyshire, Shropshire, Staffordshire, Oxfordshire* and *Worcestershire*. Passengers numbers in 1938 were around four dozen, while mailbags rarely exceeded 20.

Ships of Liverpool's famous Blue Funnel Line were rare visitors, sometimes calling at Plymouth when Naval personnel were returning from the Far East. On 2 February 1925 the *Menelaus* arrived from China with a large number of Naval ratings and officers. On 23 May 1938 the *Prometheus* landed 131 Navy and military personnel and three civilian passengers from the Far East.

Largely overshadowed by their more glamorous counterparts on the Atlantic routes, a continual stream of modestly sized cargo liners continued to call at Plymouth throughout its history as a liner port. Lines such as BI, Ellerman and Elder Dempster maintained communications with the British Empire and provided Millbay with the 'bread and butter' of its liner trade.

The liner pictured is the MODASA of the British India Steam Navigation Company. She will have departed from Bombay about four weeks previously and called at Aden, Suez, Port Said and Gibraltar. Having disembarked passengers, she is pictured unloading mail. The starboard davits of the tender, SIR JOHN HAWKINS, are swung out and the boat has been lowered – presumably providing the photographer's vantage point.

ASSOCIATED BRITISH PORTS COLLECTION SOUTHAMPTON CITY MUSEUMS

The HOBSONS BAY of the Australian Commonwealth Line in Plymouth Sound during the 1920s. Both the 'DRAKE and the 'RALEIGH are attending.
ASSOCIATED BRITISH PORTS, MILLBAY

The P&O liner ORION in Plymouth Sound on 21 January 1936.
SYDNEY GOODMAN COLLECTION

AUSTRALIA AND NEW ZEALAND

In addition to P&O in the Australian trade were the Aberdeen, Orient and Australian Commonwealth Lines. The Aberdeen Line continued to make Plymouth calls outward bound only, *en-route* from London. Ships calling were: the *Themistocles* and *Demosthenes*, which had called before the war; the *Euripides* of 1914; and the *Sophocles* and *Diogenes*, both of which were launched in 1922. On 7 April 1925 the *Diogenes* embarked a large complement of Westcountry passengers, drawn mainly from Plymouth, Callington, Liskeard, Camborne and Launceston, emigrating to Australia.

The Aberdeen Line faced competition from the Australian Government backed Commonwealth Government Line in 1916. The venture was renamed the Australian Commonwealth Line in 1922. The line operated five steamers: the *Moreton Bay, Largs Bay, Hobsons Bay, Esperance Bay* and *Jervis Bay*. The ships called occasionally at Plymouth.

The Orient Line continued calling at

Plymouth homeward bound with the popular and long serving *Orsova*, the *Ormuz* (ex-NDL ship–*Zeppelin*), the *Orvieto* and *Osterley* of 1909, and the *Ormonde* of 1911. The 20,000 ton *Orama* entered service on 15 November 1924, making her maiden voyage to Brisbane. She arrived at Plymouth on 18 February 1925 on her return maiden voyage. Calls by the Orient line decreased during the 1930s, but the *Orontes* and the renowned *Orion* of 1935, amongst others, maintained occasional calls until 1939. Prior to the *Orontes* entering service in 1929, invited guests enjoyed a cruise from Southampton to Mounts Bay in Cornwall. On the return voyage she anchored in Plymouth Sound for the night.

From 1916 New Zealand Shipping Company voyages were made via the Panama Canal. In the same year P&O gained control of the company, but the NZSCo. retained its identity. After the war the company's passenger liners included the *Paparoa, Rimutaka, Ruapehu, Ruahine,* and *Remuera,* all of which were registered at Plymouth. In 1922 the *Rotorua* (ex-Bibby Line's *Shropshire*) re-entered service, to replace the previous ship of that name which was sunk by torpedo off Start Point in 1917. Between 1928 and 1929 the New Zealand Shipping Company took delivery of three new 16,700 ton motorships, the *Rangitiki, Rangitata* and *Rangitane*. The new vessels were registered in Plymouth, but Southampton had become the intermediate port of call until 1932. In that year Plymouth was reinstated as the outbound port of call only.

JANUARY

DATE	LINER	LINE	FROM
2	THEMISTOCLES	ABERDEEN	LONDON
3	FRANCE	CGT	LE HAVRE
3	GRANTULLY CASTLE	UNION-CASTLE	E. & S. AFRICA
3	LLANSTEPHEN CASTLE	UNION-CASTLE	LONDON
3	MINNEKAHDA	AML	NY
3	ADDA	AFRICAN	W. AFRICA
4	MARGHA	BI	BOMBAY
5	VOLENDAM	NASM	NY
6	REPUBLIC	US LINES	NY
6	MACORIS	CGT	LE HAVRE
8	DAVANHA	P&O	BOMBAY
9	ZEELAND	RED STAR	NY
10	AMERICA	US LINES	NY
13	PARIS	CGT	NY
13	VAN RENSSELAER	KWIM	W. INDIES
13	RIO BRAVO	OZEAN	MEX. GULF
13	COLUMBUS	NDL	NY
14	ORSOVA	ORIENT	AUSTRALIA
14	NORMAN	UNION-CASTLE	E. & S. AFRICA
14	RYNDAM	NASM	NY
15	MANTUNA	P&O	FAR EAST
17	ABA	BRIT. & AFRICAN	W. AFRICA
17	PARIS	CGT	LE HAVRE
18	GEORGE WASHINGTON	US LINES	NY
20	FRANCE	CGT	NY
21	CALEDONIA	P&O	BOMBAY
22	ORMUZ	ORIENT	AUSTRALIA
22	MAURETANIA	CUNARD	NY
22	DUMANA	BI	CALCUTTA
24	PRESIDENT ROOSEVELT	US LINES	NY
25	FRANCE	CGT	LE HAVRE
25	MATIANA	BI	E. AFRICA
26	VEENDAM	NASM	NY
27	ANTONIA	CUNARD	NY/HALIFAX
27	ZARIA	BRIT. & AFRICAN	W. AFRICA
27	CRYNSSEN	KWIM	W. INDIES
28	CITY OF MANCHESTER	ELLERMAN HALL	KARACHI
28	STUTTGART	NDL	NY
29	MONGOLIA	P&O	AUSTRALIA
30	DEMOSTHENES	ABERDEEN	LONDON
31	ABINSI	AFRICAN	W. AFRICA
31	GRANTULLY CASTLE	UNION-CASTLE	LONDON

FEBRUARY

DATE	LINER	LINE	FROM
2	MENELAUS	BLUE FUNNEL	FAR EAST
3	PELLERIN DE LATOUCHE	CGT	LE HAVRE
3	PARIS	CGT	NY
4	NARKUNDA	P&O	BOMBAY
4	PRESIDENT HARDING	US LINES	NY
7	MINNETONKA	ATL	NY
9	AUSONIA	CUNARD	NY/HALIFAX
10	ORANJE NASSAU	KWIM	W. INDIES
10	FRANCE	CGT	NY
11	ORVIETO	ORIENT	AUSTRALIA
11	MACEDONIA	P&O	FAR EAST
12	MUNCHEN	NDL	NY
13	REPUBLIC	US LINES	NY
13	PITTSBURGH	RED STAR	NY
13	APPAM	BRIT. & AFRICAN	W. AFRICA
16	ANDANIA	CUNARD	NY
16	NIEUW AMSTERDAM	NASM	NY
18	ORAMA	ORIENT	AUSTRALIA
18	NALDERA	P&O	AUSTRALIA
19	FRANCE	CGT	LE HAVRE
19	MALDA	BI	CALCUTTA
19	GEORGE WASHINGTON	US LINES	NY
20	MACORIS	CGT	W. INDIES
23	MULBERA	BI	E. AFRICA
23	RIO PANUCO	OZEAN	MEX. GULF
26	CITY OF LONDON	ELLERMAN HALL	KARACHI
28	EURIPIDES	ABERDEEN	LONDON

Notes: 18 January – **GEORGE WASHINGTON** 147 passengers, 3,977 mailbags & $6,000,000 specie landed at Plymouth – 208 passengers & 2,162 mailbags bound for Cherbourg – 167 passengers & 2,401 mailbags bound for Bremen. **22** January – **MAURETANIA** 200 passengers & 600 mailbags landed at Plymouth.

Notes: 2 February – **MENELAUS** from China with large number of Naval ratings & officers. **3** February – **PARIS** from New York then laid up at Le Havre for 42 day overhaul. **13** February – **PITTSBURGH** first (return) voyage for Red Star, having been transferred from White Star by IMM – the parent company. She was renamed **PENNLAND** in the following year. **18** February – **ORAMA** return maiden voyage from Australia.

Liner calls for May & June 1938

MAY

DATE	LINER	LINE	FROM
1	CHINDWIN	HENDERSON	RANGOON
1	AURANIA	CUNARD-WHITE STAR	CANADA
2	QUEEN MARY	CUNARD-WHITE STAR	NY
2	VOLENDAM	NASM	NY
3	ALMEDA STAR	BLUE STAR	BUENOS AIRES
4	INKOSI	HARRISON	W. INDIES
4	COLOMBIE	CGT	W. INDIES
4	COTTICA	RNWI	NY/W. INDIES
4	STATENDAM	NASM	NY
4	ILE DE FRANCE	CGT	NY
5	NALDERA	P&O	FAR EAST
5	WORCESTERSHIRE	BIBBY	RANGOON
5	PRESIDENT ROOSEVELT	US LINES	NY
6	COLOMBIA	RNWI	W. INDIES
7	APAPA	ELDER DEMPSTER	W. AFRICA
8	AMERICAN MERCHANT	AML	NY
8	ASCANIA	CUNARD-WHITE STAR	CANADA
8	PARIS	CGT	NY
8	COLUMBUS	NDL	NY
8	DUMANA	BI	CALCUTTA
10	WASHINGTON	US LINES	NY
12	ANNIE JOHNSON	JOHNSON	VANCOUVER
12	NARKUNDA	P&O	AUSTRALIA
15	AMERICAN FARMER	AML	NY
15	CITY OF HONG KONG	ELLERMAN HALL	BOMBAY
15	VAN RENSSELAER	RNWI	W. INDIES
16	QUEEN MARY	CUNARD-WHITE STAR	NY
16	VEENDAM	NASM	NY
17	AVILA STAR	BLUE STAR	BUENOS AIRES
19	PRESIDENT HARDING	US LINES	NY
19	RANPURA	P&O	FAR EAST
19	CHESHIRE	BIBBY	RANGOON
20	MASHOBA	BI	CALCUTTA
20	ABOSSO	ELDER DEMPSTER	W. AFRICA
21	BRITANNIC	CUNARD-WHITE STAR	NY
22	AMERICAN BANKER	AML	NY
22	AUSONIA	CUNARD-WHITE STAR	CANADA
23	VENEZUELA	RNWI	W. INDIES
23	PROMETHEUS	BLUE FUNNEL	FAR EAST
26	STRATHAIRD	P&O	BRISBANE
27	NIEUW AMSTERDAM	NASM	NY
27	RANGITIKI	NZSCo.	LONDON
27	MADURA	BI	E. AFRICA
27	CARIBA	HAPAG	CENT.AMERICA
28	COLUMBUS	NDL	NY
29	AMERICAN TRADER	AML	NY
30	LANCASTRIA	CUNARD-WHITE STAR	NY/BOSTON

JUNE

DATE	LINER	LINE	FROM
1	INANDA	HARRISON	W. INDIES
2	RAWALPINDI	P&O	FAR EAST
2	PRESIDENT ROOSEVELT	US LINES	NY
3	CITY OF CANTERBURY	ELLERMAN CITY	BOMBAY
3	COSTA RICA	RNWI	W. INDIES
3	YORKSHIRE	BIBBY	RANGOON
3	PARIS	CGT	NY
3	REINA DEL PACIFICO	PSNCo.	VALPARAISO
3/4	CUBA	CGT	W. INDIES
4	ACCRA	ELDER DEMPSTER	W. AFRICA
4	AMERICAN TRADER	AML	NY
5	AURANIA	CUNARD-WHITE STAR	CANADA
6	VOLENDAM	NASM	NY
6	ORANJE NASSAU	RNWI	NY/W. INDIES
7	WASHINGTON	US LINES	NY
9	MOOLTAN	P&O	AUSTRALIA
10	STATENDAM	NASM	NY
11	AMERICAN MERCHANT	AML	NY
12	ASCANIA	CUNARD-WHITE STAR	CANADA
13	ILE DE FRANCE	CGT	NY
13	QUEEN MARY	CUNARD-WHITE STAR	NY
14	ANDALUCIA STAR	BLUE STAR	BUENOS AIRES
16	PRESIDENT HARDING	US LINES	NY
16	CORFU	P&O	FAR EAST
17	NIEUW AMSTERDAM	NASM	NY
18	MULBERA	BI	CALCUTTA
18	CHAMPLAIN	CGT	NY
18	ABA	ELDER DEMPSTER	W. AFRICA
18	AUSONIA	CUNARD-WHITE STAR	CANADA
18	COLUMBUS	NDL	NY
19	DERBYSHIRE	BIBBY	RANGOON
19	SIMON BOLIVAR	RNWI	W. INDIES
22	MATIANA	BI	E. AFRICA
22	CAP ARCONA	HAMBURG SUD	BUENOS AIRES
22	MANHATTAN	US LINES	NY
23	CITY OF BENARES	ELLERMAN CITY	BOMBAY
23	STRATHALLAN	P&O	AUSTRALIA
23	CORDILLERA	HAPAG	W. INDIES
24	RANGITATA	NZSCo.	LONDON
25	APAPA	ELDER DEMPSTER	W. AFRICA
25	ALAUNIA	CUNARD-WHITE STAR	CANADA
26	AMERICAN TRADER	AML	NY
27	VEENDAM	NASM	NY
27	STUYVESANT	RNWI	NY/W. INDIES
28	INKOSI	HARRISON	W. INDIES
28	DE GRASSE	CGT	NY
29	ILE DE FRANCE	CGT	NY
30	PRESIDENT ROOSEVELT	US LINES	NY

Notes: **4** May – **STATENDAM** first trans-Atlantic crossing since cruising from NY for 5 months. **10** May – **WASHINGTON** landed 134 passengers at Cobh, 243 passengers & 1,394 mailbags at Plymouth, 194 passengers for Le Havre & 164 for Hamburg. **16** May – **QUEEN MARY** landed 482 passengers & 2000 mailbags. **21** May – **BRITANNIC** first visit to Plymouth. **23** May – **VENEZUELA** making her last Plymouth call prior to withdrawal & breaking. **23** May – **PROMETHEUS** 131 naval & military personnel from far east. **27** May – **NIEUW AMSTERDAM** return maiden voyage.

Notes: **13** June – **ILE DE FRANCE** arrived 7.20am, landed 171 passengers, 68 mailbags & departed 9.15am. **QUEEN MARY** arrived 7.45am, landed 406 passengers, 2,100 mailbags & departed 10.15am.

CHAPTER FIVE
ATTENDING A LINER

SIGNALS

In the mid 19th century a lookout was stationed on Plymouth Hoe, in the position occupied today by the small, octagonal, castellated limestone structure in front of Smeaton's Tower. The view of Cawsand Bay and the western entrance to Plymouth Sound is largely obscured from Millbay by Drake's Island. A lookout positioned on the Hoe offered some advanced warning of incoming mail ships. The octagonal lookout shelter was built c.1870 with windows on the seaward facing sides. The design echoes the architecture of the octagonal Customs office at Millbay Pier and it is possible that signals were exchanged between lookouts on the flat roofs of the two buildings. The Ordnance Survey of 1914 still described this structure as a lookout.

THE RAME HEAD SIGNAL STATION.

Chairman :
W. T. LEAMAN.

Hon. Secretary & Treasurer :
D. G. HOPPINS.

DOCK OFFICE,
GREAT WESTERN DOCKS,
PLYMOUTH.

In 1890 the port's shipping agents and the Great Western Railway formed a committee, to operate a signal station at Rame Head, overlooking the approaches to Plymouth Sound. From this headland ships could be sighted in the English Channel at a distance of 20 miles. Early in 1932 the Rame Head Signal Station Committee leased another building at Rame Head from the Admiralty and installed a wire-

The letterheading of the GWR's and Plymouth shipping agents' Committee for the Rame Head Signal Station.
DOUGLASS HOPPINS COLLECTION

The members and signalman of the Rame Head Signal Station Committee, photographed outside the signal station in 1927. Standing, left to right: Signalman Williams; Mr Nicholls; Mr W. T. Leaman – Chairman of the Signal Station Committee and the Cunard (later Cunard White Star) agent at Plymouth; Mr Cockram; Mr Kerr; Mr Huish. Seated: Mr Mullard; Mr D. G. Hoppins - Secretary and Treasurer of the Signal Station Committee and Chief Clerk at Millbay; Mr Gould; Mr Davis – shipping and Lloyds agent at Plymouth.

H. A. CLEAR,
DOUGLASS HOPPINS COLLECTION

The signal station building at Rame Head has been altered and now serves as a Coastguard lookout.

A. KITTRIDGE

less directional beacon for the assistance of ships making the port. The ¼kw Marconi wireless beacon had a range of over 20 miles and was operated in fog or at the request of shipping companies. The call sign of the station, GPM, was automatically repeated at a rate of 75 letters per minute for 50 seconds. There followed a 10 second pause and the signal was terminated by the call sign being sent once only. There were three minutes silence before repetition. The cost of equipping and running the station was borne largely by the GWR, but some shipping companies and Plymouth Chamber of Commerce also contributed.

Prior notice of a ship's arrival was also forthcoming from the Lloyd's Signal Station on the Lizard. Before the advent of ship to shore radio telegraphy, ships were required to sail or steam close enough to the Lizard to signal their identity to the lookouts. At night the signals took the form of a pyrotechnic display – Private Night Signals – known as company signals. The Aberdeen Line, for instance, displayed a red pyrotechnic light near the stern, followed by a roman candle throwing up three groups of balls to a height not exceeding 50 feet and each group consisting of a red, white and blue ball. HAPAG, while off the Isles of Scilly, Lizard and Plymouth, signalled identity at night with three roman candles in succession at the stern, each throwing to a height not exceeding 50 feet, seven stars: white, red, blue, white, red, blue, white. NDL showed two pyrotechnic lights simultaneously, each changing from blue to red. Most shipping companies registered their own distinctive code, many of them quite complex. The lookouts' nights might thus have

been enlivened but one can imagine some frantic moments noting the display and then searching the code books.

In 1899 Marconi established radio communication between the American Line's *St Paul* and a shore station at the Needles. Within two years NDL's express trans-Atlantic liners were fitted with telegraphs and wireless communication was quickly established throughout the shipping world. Following the development of radio telegraphy, a wireless station was established on the Lizard, a quarter of a mile west of the Lloyd's Signal Station.

The estimated time of arrival of a liner at Plymouth was determined weeks, perhaps months in advance. This was the case ever since steamships entered service because, by comparison with sailing ships, they were less prone to the vagaries of the weather. When radio was introduced during the first decade of the 20th century the availability of shipping intelligence became almost immediate. From the time a colonial liner left port, a stream of radio communications advised shipping agents at ports-of-call of her position. Notification of arrival time, together with details of passengers, mails and specie to be landed, became more precise as the liner neared Plymouth. Trans-Atlantic liners were in radio contact from, or soon after, departure from New York and their estimated time of arrival at Plymouth was continually updated throughout the voyage. On the morning of Sunday 6 November 1910 Orlando Davis & Co., the Plymouth shipping agents for NDL, received a telegraph message from Captain Cuppers of the *Kaiser Wilhelm II*, stating 'Will probably arrive at 5.30am on Monday 7th'. The Captain also advised the agents of passengers and mails to be disembarked at Plymouth – 84 passengers, 1,308 mailbags and specie to the value $218,592. Included amongst the VIP's landing at Plymouth were members of the Astor family. The liner duly dropped anchor at 5.33 am on the 7th.

ANCHORAGE AND PILOTS

The choice between anchoring in Cawsand Bay or inside the Breakwater was a decision for the liner captain, subject to weather conditions, depth of water available inside the Breakwater and the advice of the pilot. More protection was

The Lloyds' Signal Station on the Lizard. Flying from the mast is the signal pennant 'Answer and Code'.

A. KITTRIDGE COLLECTION

The Lizard, Lloyd's Signal Station

offered inside the Breakwater, but if sea conditions were suitable it could be expedient to anchor in Cawsand Bay. Some ships, particularly cargo liners, used the designated merchant vessel anchorage off Jennycliff. The pilotage of any ship demands the confidence of the captain with the pilot and CGT, amongst other lines, would request particular Plymouth pilots for their ships.

The anchorage of Plymouth Sound provided an average 30 feet depth at low water, with an average rise of tide of 13 feet. The limits of the port extend to an imaginary line drawn from Rame Head in the west, to the Great Mew Stone in the east. Pilotage rates for steamships were based on draft and in 1936 ranged from 2s. 6d. (approximately. 13p) per foot–draft 10 feet and under; to 3s. 9d. (approximately. 19p) per foot–draft 25 feet and over. Ships calling to land or embark passengers or mails were allowed a 25% reduction on these charges. The pilot might stay on board while a liner was at anchor, as he was required to advise on the anchorage and to swing the ship prior to departure.

Only on rare occasions did the elements conspire to render the transfer of passengers too dangerous at Plymouth. On 11 February 1914 the *Olympic* arrived in rough seas. Of the four tenders dispatched to the liner only the *Sir Richard Grenville* was able to complete her task of taking off the baggage. The *Sir Walter Raleigh*, *Sir Francis Drake* and *Smeaton* were unable to disembark their respective passengers, mails and specie, which was taken on to Le Havre and subsequently Southampton.

PORT OFFICIALS AND THE PRESS

As the tenders prepared to leave Millbay they were joined by various personnel, each with a specific interest in the liner. In an official capacity were Immigration and Customs officials, the Port Health Officer, Post Office staff to supervise the transfer of the mails, a representative of the appropriate shipping agency, and a consul – if the ship was foreign flagged. On special occasions, such as a maiden voyage or an inaugural call, representatives of the railway, docks, Plymouth Chamber of Commerce and City might attend. When the CGT's *Lafayette* called on her maiden voyage on 18 May 1930,

the Mayor of Plymouth, Alderman Churchwald, went out to meet CGT officials aboard the ship. Other regulars aboard the tenders included a newspaper vendor selling the latest edition of *The Times* and additional Post Office personnel to set up a temporary post desk aboard the ship.

News reporters and photographers also joined the tenders, their reports appearing in the local press or through the Press Association for national publication when the story warranted. Local reporters included Walter Taylor and Crispin Gill – relief Shipping Editors of the *Western Morning News* in the 1920s and '30s respectively; Martin Endel – Shipping Editor of the *Western Daily Mercury* and from 1922 Shipping Editor of the *Western Morning News*; and Rufus Endel, Martin's son – a freelance journalist. The outline voyage log of each mail ship was reproduced in the *Western Morning News*. Most of the information was gleaned

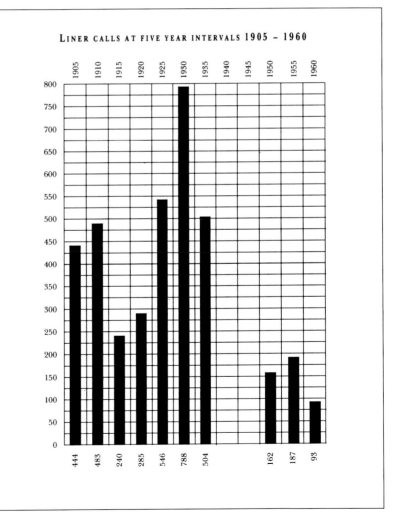

LINER CALLS AT FIVE YEAR INTERVALS 1905 – 1960

Port officials, shipping agents and a newspaper vendor board the P&O liner RANCHI in Cawsand Bay in April 1927.
ASSOCIATED BRITISH PORTS COLLECTION SOUTHAMPTON CITY MUSEUMS

Chaplin, Vivien Leigh, Marlene Dietrich, Mary Pickford, and later: Tony Curtis, Ertha Kitt, Boris Karloff etc. All offered useful column inches for hard pressed editors on a slow day. The Hollywood hype found an avid audience in Britain and little trouble was experienced by Plymouth's reporters in interviewing international stars, even though most of the celebrities remained aboard ship and continued their voyage to the Continent and Southampton to ensure maximum press coverage. Passenger Lists and Press Releases were compiled by the publicity departments of the shipping companies for the benefit of ships' Pursers. In turn similar lists were distributed to the press by the shipping agents – any resulting publicity surrounding the VIPs on the liners represented a free endorsement for the line.

In the early years of the century the photographer Frank of Plymouth travelled aboard the tenders to record shipping at Plymouth and produce some of the GWR's official photographs. Later Cyril H. Gill photographed shipping for the press. Dermot Fitzgerald also photographed liners for the *Western Morning News*. After the Second World War, Robert Chapman, a Plymouth photographer, covered CGT's arrivals for the *London Evening Standard* – throughout her career CGT's *Ile de France* was the favoured ship of artists, writers and actors.

Occasionally Special Branch officers might join the tender. Security was tight on 2 February 1929 when P&O's *Rajputana* arrived at Plymouth. T. E. Lawrence was aboard returning from a controversial visit to troubled Afghanistan. He was kept away from waiting newsmen and taken off the liner by the Naval Duty Officer's pinnace and landed at RAF Mount Batten. Lawrence was then driven to Newton Abbot to catch the London train.

from log sheets, which, aboard trans-Atlantic liners in particular, included the daily speeds and distances travelled. These logs were produced by the Navigating Officer and issued aboard ship for benefit of the passengers. Collectively the newspaper reporters interviewed many world statesmen and politicians including Cecil Rhodes, General Allenby, Lloyd George, Winston Churchill and General Smuts. There were aristocrats and rich middle class capitalists, writers, actors, adventurers and sportsmen – a rich source of copy for the rather mistitled 'Shipping' Editor. The consensus among his contemporaries and successors suggests that Martin Endel was foremost amongst the shipping reporters, having gained the confidence of many ships' Pursers.

Between the wars the full effect of the Hollywood publicity machine was experienced and 'movie stars' aspired to VIP status: Charlie

First aboard the liner would be an officer of the Port Health Authority, with a questionnaire to be completed by the master. Ships arriving from Africa or the east, having called at ports where there were infectious diseases, might be 'suspected' and were liable to examination by the Port Medical Officer. To request the Port Medical Officer a ship flew the LIM international code flags. A yellow Q flag indicated a healthy ship and subject to the Port Health

Passengers from the MAURETANIA catch up with the news aboard the SMEATON at Fishguard in August 1909. Passengers continuing their voyage aboard the liner could send letters from a temporary Post Office desk which was set up while the tender was alongside.
BRIAN JACKSON COLLECTION

PASSENGERS AND BAGGAGE

Once the initial port formalities were completed aboard the liner, passengers disembarked onto the tender. Baggage followed, being stowed on the after deck and covered with a tarpaulin if it was raining. When a large number of passengers were being landed a special baggage tender was employed. Sheltered accommodation aboard the tenders was plentiful and the saloons were warm and comfortable. A licensed refreshment bar was always open aboard the tenders when they were on passenger duty. The trip to Millbay only occupied 10 to 15 minutes, but the duration of disembarkation from the liner added to the time spent aboard the tender.

Liner passengers were landed on Millbay Pier, only a short walk beneath the awning to the waiting room. The waiting rooms were completely refurbished and enlarged in 1936. The resulting bright, stylish but simple decor was in complete contrast to the heavy, Victorian interior that existed before. There was a railway booking office, telegraph office, licensed refreshment bar, newsagent, travel agent and Bureau de Change, all located within the waiting room area.

Meanwhile, the baggage was taken by the baggage railway to the Customs inspection tables on the ground floors of warehouses 3, 4 and 5. The luggage was sorted under the initial letters of the respective owners prior to Customs examination. The examination was undertaken by GWR staff under Customs supervision. The baggage of each passenger had a consecutive number affixed and receipts bearing corresponding numbers were given to the passengers to claim their luggage. In the 1870s there was a charge of 6d. per passenger, inclusive of all their baggage, for landing at Plymouth by tender. This toll was later transferred to the shipping lines in the form of a charter fee, the cost to the passenger being absorbed or included in the ticket price by the shipping line. When customs and immigration procedures were completed, the passengers were free to depart. The Army and Navy Stores' Plymouth Depot, in Union Street, offered to supervise the landing, clearing, forwarding or warehousing of liner passengers'

baggage, leaving them free to proceed by rail without further delay.

Railway tickets could be purchased in advance aboard the ship. Pursers aboard trans-Atlantic liners were responsible for ordering

Trans-Atlantic passengers in the Waiting Room during the 1950s.
ASSOCIATED BRITISH PORTS, MILLBAY

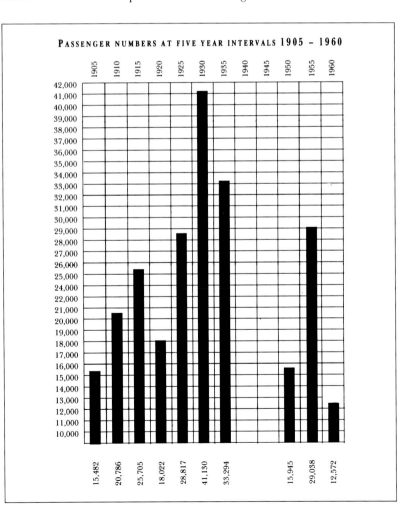

PASSENGER NUMBERS AT FIVE YEAR INTERVALS 1905 – 1960

1905	1910	1915	1920	1925	1930	1935	1940	1945	1950	1955	1960
15,482	20,786	25,705	18,022	28,817	41,130	33,294			15,945	29,038	12,572

Luggage from the ADDA being carried ashore on 12 March 1927. In the foreground is the 2 feet 6 inches gauge baggage railway.

DOUGLASS HOPPINS COLLECTION

Traces of the baggage railway are still in evidence in this 1988 photograph. In the background are the Customs Office, pier gates and Pier Hotel building.

A. KITTRIDGE

Plymouth in 1903, the L&SWR at Ocean Quay introduced Ocean Special trains, with rakes of carriages fitted to a very high standard. The GWR meanwhile continued to use first and third class stock from their existing pool.

Between 1929–1930 the GWR experimented in using some Pullman carriages on their ocean liner trains. In 1931 a special set of Ocean Saloons (or Super Saloons depending where they were used) were introduced. Three of these coaches nos 9111, 9112 and 9113 were first used for guests of CGT who were travelling from Le Havre to London on the occasion of the maiden voyage of the *Colombie*. The saloons were fitted with brackets for name-boards, which in subsequent years bore the legends 'French Line via Plymouth', 'Cunard Line Boat Train' and 'United States Line via Plymouth'. Permission was granted to name the saloons after members of the Royal Family:

No 9111 – *King George*
No 9112 – *Queen Mary*
No 9113 – *Prince of Wales*
No 9114 – *Duke of York*
No 9115 – *Duke of Gloucester*
No 9116 – *Duchess of York*
No 9117 – *Princess Royal*
No 9118 – *Princess Elizabeth*

passenger trains at Plymouth, Le Havre /Cherbourg and Southampton. Passenger numbers for Ocean Specials at Millbay were radioed ahead to the shipping agent, who booked the appropriate number of carriages. In their attempt to retain the American Line's passenger traffic, when the line started calling at

The Baggage Inspection Rooms at Millbay. The first two pictures, taken in 1906, show Baggage Inspection Room No 1. The baggage railway runs into the room and loops around the inspection tables, to rejoin the railway outside.

In the second picture baggage railway trucks can be seen at the entrance and exit doors. Note also the weighing scales in the centre.

The third photograph shows Baggage Inspection Room No 2 in 1906. Note the different roof and pillars. There was no baggage railway inside this room, an indication perhaps that it was converted for use as an inspection room at a later date than room No 1.

DOUGLASS HOPPINS COLLECTION

Passengers from Australia claiming their luggage in Baggage Inspection Room No 1 during the early 1960s.
ASSOCIATED BRITISH PORTS, MILLBAY

Passengers at the docks station on East Quay on 1 May 1931. In the absence of a platform, wooden steps were needed to board the train.
ASSOCIATED BRITISH PORTS COLLECTION SOUTHAMPTON CITY MUSEUMS

The names were applied in large gold letters along the carriage sides.

Railway passenger carriages were shunted down to Millbay Pier. The rails ran to the buffer stops, located beneath the awning at the southern end of East Quay. Locomotives in use at Millbay included the 1392 class 0-6-0 tank engines. These were ex-Cornwall Minerals Railway engines, converted to saddle tanks. In 1910 new drawings were produced based on these engines and the resulting saddle tank

locomotives were numbered 1361–5. They were mainly allocated to Plymouth becoming a familiar sight in Millbay Docks, usually coupled to a shunters truck. Passenger and mail carriages were marshalled into trains by the shunting engines, but taken out of Millbay by mainline engines – the only restricted locomotive class were the 'double red' classified Kings.

In the last years of the liner trade, coaches were still shunted down to Millbay Pier for liner passengers to board, but were then hauled up to North Road Station and attached to a timetabled London train.

OCEAN MAILS AND SPECIE

The Post Office regained control of the Ocean Mails from the Admiralty in 1867. Soon after, the sorting of the West India Mail, previously undertaken aboard the mailship, was transferred to a Travelling Post Office (TPO) which ran from Millbay – the official title being, Plymouth & Bristol TPO (Foreign Mails). The Ocean Mails trains were run as specials, i.e. not timetabled. They ran under various titles indicating the mail they carried, e.g. Special Cape Mails, Special West India Mails etc.

In 1895 four 40 feet Passenger Brake Vans, numbers 862–5, and a letter sorting carriage, were available to make up Ocean Mails trains.

Mailbags and cases of parcels were landed regularly by the RMSPCo., P&O, Castle, NZSCo. PSNCo and Union lines. Compared to later years each call offered modest loads, comprising anything from 10 to 150 mailbags and up to 100 cases of parcels.

In 1910 there was a marked increase in mail traffic, with both the American Line and NDL regularly landing in excess of 1,500 mailbags on each visit and White Star's New York liners averaging around 400 bags per call. By 1915 six additional vans were available for Ocean Mails trains – four stowage vans nos 821–4 (built in 1904), and two letter sorting carriages, nos 836 and 837. Carriage no. 837 was a slip coach and carried mails for the north. The coach was slipped from the main train at Bristol while it was still moving. The pre-First World War peak, from figures available, was in 1913, when 219,691 mailbags were landed.

In 1925 CGT was landing up to 3,500 mail

Post Office staff and port officials gather aboard the mail tender CHESHIRE prior to attending an American Line steamer, c. 1905.

A. KITTRIDGE COLLECTION

bags per call, the United States Lines ranged between 500 and 4,500, NDL over 2,000 and Red Star up to 3,000 bags on each visit. The peak year between the wars was 1930 when 307,912 mailbags were landed. These figures declined in the '30s, but the United States Line and their subsidiary American Merchant Line continued landing around 1,000 bags on each of their combined twice weekly visits. In 1938 Cunard's *Queen Mary* was landing the largest numbers of mailbags, over 2,000 per call. From 1925 the sorting of mail aboard Ocean Mails

The CHESHIRE alongside the KAISER WILHELM DER GROSSE c. 1905. The mailbags slide down ramps and are sorted into groups aboard the tender.

BRITISH RAILWAYS

Mailbags from the MAURETANIA aboard the SIR WALTER RALEIGH. Note the bags sliding down the ramps, the safety net slung beneath the ramps and the wicker hurdles which made up into baskets and helped divide the mail.

DOUGLASS HOPPINS COLLECTION

Aboard the SMEATON at Fishguard in August 1909. Some wicker baskets have been erected. Once loaded they were lifted off by crane.

BRIAN JACKSON COLLECTION

trains was discontinued and a number of 70 feet Post Office Stowage Vans were developed for the ocean traffic. Nos 1202–5 were built to the limits of the loading gauge and fitted with six wheeled bogies.

The all time peak year for ocean mail was in 1949, when, although the liner trade was in decline, 437,295 bags were landed. By 1962 the figure had dwindled to just 2,872. The carriage of mail from Millbay on special trains continued until the port was closed to such traffic in 1963.

The mails were usually taken off the liner by a second tender. If space was available on deck a rough sorting of mailbags was undertaken before the tender reached Millbay. When the quantity was so great that it took up the entire deck space, two tenders might be dispatched – one to take the London bound mail and the second to embark mails for Bristol and the North (the division being having been made in the mail room aboard the liner).

Once the tender was moored in Millbay the bags were handled by dockers under Post Office supervision and Customs observation, being carried to the waiting Ocean Mails train. In 1927 the process was hastened by the installation of an electric conveyor belt on East Quay. One end of the conveyor was positioned over the bows of the tender and onto the forward promenade deck. The other end ran straight into the waiting carriages.

The quantity of mail always increased significantly at Christmas. The greatest logistical problem was caused by the massive increase in numbers of parcels, as each one had to be opened for Customs examination – on 18 December 1931 the *President Roosevelt* alone landed 5,000 parcels. Additional accommodation for parcels examination was provided in the end baggage warehouse. In 1931 the room was specially fitted out for use in the two weeks prior to and two weeks after Christmas. Sixty temporary Post Office staff were employed for the four week duration. It was the duty of the

Post Office to open each parcel. The contents were exposed upon their original wrapping and passed down the long tables for examination by Custom Officers. About 80% were assessed for duty. In many cases the duty had been pre-paid by the consignee, otherwise a label was attached for the duty to be collected from the addressee. P&O ships from India attracted particular attention as many parcels contained tea or spices subject to duty. The parcel continued down the table to be retied and dispatched.

Valuable consignments of specie were a regular feature at Millbay. $6,000,000 specie was landed from the *George Washington* in January 1925. On 25 August 1938 the *Aquitania* made a

special call at Plymouth *en-route* to New York, to embark £5,000,000 gold (Plymouth was preferred to Southampton for security reasons). Seemingly contrary to recollections of universal honesty which prevailed in the 'good old days', the GWR deemed it prudent to provide specially constructed bullion vans. No 820 of 1907 was rostered at Millbay. It was 36 feet long, built of steel throughout, with windows and doors on one side only, each door was fitted with double locks. However, some naïvety is apparent when reading contemporary announcements in the local newspapers of the imminent arrival of large quantities of specie. In the last weeks before war broke out in 1939, westbound Dutch and French lines collected large quanti-

Hauling up the gangway after Post Office officials, Customs officers and U.S. Mails have transferred from the United States Lines' GEORGE WASHINGTON in April 1927.

ASSOCIATED BRITISH PORTS
COLLECTION
SOUTHAMPTON CITY MUSEUMS

Flying a Royal Mail pennant and the houseflag of NDL, the CHESHIRE departs from a liner in Cawsand Bay.

DOUGLASS HOPPINS COLLECTION

The CHESHIRE, laden with mailbags, moored at Trinity Pier.

A. KITTRIDGE COLLECTION

ties of gold bullion from Plymouth; 89 boxes (over £1,000,000) aboard the *Noordam*, 129 boxes (£1,500,000) aboard the *Ile de France*, and two consignments, each of over £2,000,000 gold, by the *Normandie*.

SECOND WORLD WAR

On 25 August 1939, over a week before war was declared, the tenders *Sir Francis Drake*, *Sir Walter Raleigh* and *Sir Richard Grenville* were

Photographed later, dockers have reduced the pile of mailbags aboard the CHESHIRE and are carrying them to the mail train on East Quay. The leading vehicles are two of the 70 feet Ocean Mails vans, which introduced in 1904. On the right, mostly hidden behind Trinity Pier, is the slip coach, No. 837, built in 1905 so that mail for Bristol and the north could be slipped at Bedminster while the train was still moving.

DOUGLASS HOPPINS COLLECTION

chartered for examination service at Plymouth – inspecting non-belligerent shipping. The *Sir John Hawkins* remained available for tendering but served as relief vessel for examination service. Further reporting of shipping movements in the press stopped on 25 August. The following day the Admiralty assumed control of all British merchant shipping.

At 11.00am on 3 September war was declared against Germany. Seventeen minutes later all HM ships received the signal – renowned for its concise brevity – 'Total Germany'. P&O's *Chitral* and Harrison's *Inanda* arrived at Plymouth on 24 August, the last before Admiralty restrictions were imposed. Harrison's *Inkosi* was *en-route* from the West Indies when war was declared, she completed her voyage under blackout conditions. In 1940 both the *Inkosi* and *Inanda* were so badly damaged in air raids over London that they never entered passenger service again. Only a few

neutral liners, overtaken by events whilst *en-route*, remained to be attended. Other liners caught out by the declaration of war included NDL's *Columbus* – a faithful Plymouth visitor. Her career ended dramatically on 19 December 1939, while she was making a trans-Atlantic dash for Germany. She was scuttled by her crew, 300 miles off the Virginia coast, to avoid capture by the destroyer HMS *Hyperion*. Her fleet sister, the *Bremen*, proved successful in her bid to reach home, only to be irreparably

The SIR FRANCIS DRAKE and the SIR WALTER RALEIGH at Trinity Pier in March 1927, loaded with mail. The mailbags are real enough, but the shot is posed and was part of an official set taken when the electric conveyor belt was introduced. The forward deckrails on the tenders' promenade decks have been adapted to take the conveyor belt. The conveyor itself was already in location, adjacent to Princess Royal Pier, when this picture was taken. The purpose of the set of photographs was to record the old and new methods of unloading mails at Millbay.
ASSOCIATED BRITISH PORTS
COLLECTION
SOUTHAMPTON CITY MUSEUMS

A second picture taken on the same day showing unloading by hand. Three Post Office staff are supervising.
DOUGLASS HOPPINS COLLECTION

This third shot of the 'old' method of handling mailbags rather gives the game away as the new conveyor belt support and cylindrical counterbalance can be seen in the background, on Princess Royal Pier.

DOUGLASS HOPPINS COLLECTION

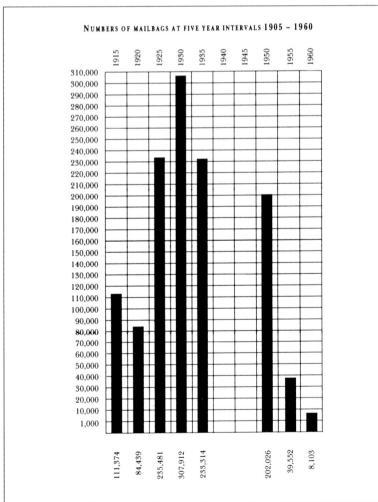

NUMBERS OF MAILBAGS AT FIVE YEAR INTERVALS 1905 – 1960

1915	1920	1925	1930	1935	1940	1945	1950	1955	1960
111,374	84,439	235,481	307,912	233,314			202,026	39,552	8,103

damaged by fire in 1941.

On the Continent the 'Phoney War' – an early period of relative inactivity between the belligerents – was contrasted by early engagements in the North Sea and Atlantic. P&O's *Rawalpindi* was converted to an Armed Merchant Cruiser (AMC) during the the very first weeks of the war. On 23 November 1939 she encountered the German battlecruisers, *Scharnhorst* and *Gneisenau*. Escape was hopeless, attack was preferred to surrender. After a heroic but futile action the *Rawalpindi* was sunk by the *Scharnhorst*. The German battlecruisers were engaged in distracting British naval patrols so that the *Bremen* and other ships could slip through the Denmark Strait or Faroes Gap to Germany.

BI's *Domala* was bombed and destroyed off the Isle of Wight on 2 March 1940. The Orient Line's *Orama* was sunk by the heavy cruiser *Admiral Hipper* during the Norwegian campaign in 1940. The 11,000 ton, twin funnelled *City of Benares*' short career ended in disaster. Launched in 1936 the Ellerman liner was sunk by a U-boat on 17 September 1940, whilst *enroute* to Canada with evacuee children. 248 people were lost, including 77 children.

The *Jervis Bay*, of the Aberdeen & Commonwealth Line, was taken over by the

The lights and bustle of a night time liner arrival added to the air of excitement at Millbay. Unfortunately photographs of these regular events are rare. This picture shows the conveyor in use at night and serves to illustrate the level of activity demanded at any hour during the night, following the arrival of a liner.
DOUGLASS HOPPINS COLLECTION

hard pressed to keep pace with the huge losses being suffered by the merchant navy. The Blue Star Line's entire passenger fleet – the *Andalucia Star, Avila Star, Avelona Star* and *Arandora Star* – was sunk by U-boats. Elder Dempster's *Accra* was sunk by U-boat, as was the *Adda* and the *Abosso*. The *Apapa* was bombed and sunk.

The British merchant fleet suffered the greatest losses, but it didn't suffer alone. Having just been converted as a troop ship CGT's *Normandie* was destroyed by a combination of fire and incompetence in New York in 1942. In May 1940 NASM's *Statendam* was hit by bombs and destroyed by fire. KNSM suffered huge losses, only two of their seven passenger liners survived the war. On 13 May 1940, whilst evacuating Jewish children, the *Van Rensselaer* struck a mine at Ijmuiden and sank in the harbour entrance. The *Costa Rica* was sunk on 27 April 1941 whilst *en-route* to Crete with 2,800 British troops aboard, fortunately there was no loss of life. NDL's old liner, the *Stuttgart* was converted to a hospital ship. In 1943 she was hit during an allied air raid on

Gdynia – there was considerable loss of life and the wreck, along with many bodies, was later sunk at sea. One of the greatest tragedies at sea befell Hamburg-Süd's *Cap Arcona*. In May 1945 she was attacked and sunk by the RAF in the Bay of Lübeck. Over 5,000 lost their lives, most of them were concentration camp prisoners being transferred to Germany from Poland.

When the war ended in 1945, losses suffered by the Allies' merchant navies from enemy action totalled 4,786 ships. Approximately 30,000 merchant seamen were killed. Ships, shipping lines and seamen of many nationalities had suffered enormous losses.

Shipyards enjoyed a post-war boom and in a relatively short time most of the fleets, including the resilient German lines, began to operate again. Inevitably, with so many ships lost in the war, the post-war fleets were transformed, and new lines appeared. But any hopes of returning to pre-war figures were soon dashed – the days of ocean liner travel were drawing to a close. Within 17 years of the end of the war, Plymouth would be closed as a passenger and mail liner port.

570

PLYMOUTH,

M.. 194

Dr. to THE GREAT WESTERN RAILWAY COMPANY.

Cheques and Postal Orders should be crossed and made Payable to the Order of the Great Western Railway Company.
The Company's Adhesive receipt forms must always be used by Collectors in giving receipts.

DATE	SS..		RATE	AMOUNT
	To Hire of Tender			
	,, ,, ,, Pole Fenders			
	Mails			
	Parcels Post			
	Superintendence, etc.			
	Specie, Bars			
	,, Kegs			
	,, Boxes			
	Registered Baggage Plymouth to Paddington Pkges.			
	Labour Charges ....Men in Sound			
	,, Registered Baggage ....Men			
	Insurance Stamps—Health			
	,, Unemployment			
	Excess Luggage per cwt.			
	Percentage			

30 bks., 250 lvs.—Est. 679   7/45 (8).

A GWR invoice to the shipping agent for the hire of liner tenders at Plymouth.

AUTHOR'S COLLECTION.

CHAPTER SIX

THE END OF THE LINER TRADE

1945 – 1963

Merchant shipping worldwide suffered as a consequence of the war. Fleets were devastated and their remaining ships dislocated. By 1945 there was a huge backlog of shipyard work. Few, if any, of the belligerents' surviving passenger vessels could re-enter civilian service without major refits. Passenger lines were faced with the additional problem of competition by airlines.

AIRLINES

Ever since the 1930s Imperial Airways' Handley Page airliners had made incursions into the carriage of overseas mail. By 1939 mails from New Zealand, Australia, Burma, Ceylon, Egypt, Hong Kong, India, the Malay States, North Borneo, Sarawak, the Straits Settlements and many African colonies, were being transported by air.

The first scheduled trans-Atlantic flight, Pan Am Boeing 314 Flying Boat the *Yankee Clipper*, landed at Shannon Airport, Foynes, on 28 June 1939. Late in 1940 BOAC operated from Poole Harbour to Foynes, Lisbon and across the Atlantic.

The sight of flying boats landing in Plymouth Sound had been commonplace ever since an air station was established at Mount Batten during the First World War. On West Pier, in Sutton Harbour, there is a bronze tablet commemorating the first ever trans-Atlantic flight in 1919, by U.S. Navy Curtiss Flying Boat NC4, which arrived at Plymouth after a 25 hour flight via Newfoundland, the Azores and Lisbon.

On the outskirts of Plymouth, at Roborough, a hangar and landing place was completed at the end of 1931. Six hangars, workshops and administrative buildings were proposed for the airport development. Mr D. G. Hoppins, Chief Clerk at Millbay, noted the possibility of trans-Atlantic liner passengers landing at Plymouth and proceeding by air to their final European destination.

The Plan for Plymouth – for the rebuilding of the City after the war – published in 1943, suggested developing a passenger seaplane base at Plymouth. Two sites were considered; Plymouth Sound – where it was thought that civil flights might conflict with RAF Mount Batten, or St John's Lake – between Millbrook and Torpoint on the Cornish side of the River Tamar. Construction of a barrage at the entrance to the lake (tidal creek) was envisaged, to provide water runways of over 1000 yards at all states of the tide. It was suggested that a ferry service would convey passengers directly to Plymouth, presumably landing at Millbay for Customs and the railway.

However, the development of land aircraft quickly overtook all such water based schemes. In 1945 the last trans-Atlantic flying boat was withdrawn. Douglas DC4 land planes were introduced and by 1946 TWA's land plane routes spanned half the world. Tourists from both sides of the Atlantic were switching to air travel, catered for largely by all-tourist DC6 aircraft. In 1956 the Douglas DC7C offered non-stop trans-Atlantic flight. Meanwhile Pan Am ordered a fleet of 48 jet engined air liners for the trans-Atlantic routes and in October 1958 introduced the first commercial jet aircraft on trans-Atlantic service. In June 1963, the year Plymouth was closed as an ocean liner port, long range Boeing 707 intercontinental aircraft entered service.

It was therefore against the devastation of war and the development of air travel, that passenger shipping lines endeavoured to re-establish themselves after the war.

For the first time since 1939 Capt. Roberts of the Royal Mail Line's DRINA was able to steam through the western approaches with his navigation lights showing and without fear of submarine attack. Basking in the early morning sun, the DRINA is pictured in Plymouth Sound on 19 June 1945 homeward bound from Montevideo.

Launched from Harland & Wolff's Belfast yard in July 1944, the DRINA was designed to carry passengers and meat from Argentina. The trappings of war – guns, grey paint and Carley Floats – have yet to be removed. The tug's stern is possibly that of the RMAS tug CAMEL, which attended the liner in the absence of the GWR tenders. Amongst the DRINA's 25 passengers landing at Millbay were young British expatriates intent upon careers in the armed forces and medical professions.

ASSOCIATED BRITISH PORTS COLLECTION
SOUTHAMPTON CITY MUSEUMS

EARLY POST WAR LINE CALLS

At 3pm on 8 May 1945, Winston Churchill broadcast to the nation that the war in Europe had ended. Once the euphoria of VE Day was over, the mammoth task of demobilisation began. In Scapa Flow the *Sir John Hawkins* finished her war service and remained at moorings until officially released on 24 July 1945. In the same month the *Sir Francis Drake* returned to Plymouth.

Meanwhile, on 19 June, the first post war liner call was made by the Royal Mail Lines' *Drina*, from Montevideo. She landed 25 passengers and 24 mailbags. As no tender was available the Admiralty supplied the paddle tug *Camel* from Devonport Dockyard. Newsmen accompanying the tug were refused permission to board the *Drina* owing to wartime controls which were still in force. However, Mr. R. H. Bate, the Dock Manager, officially welcomed Capt. W. H. Roberts,

who promptly side-stepped the regulations by being interviewed aboard the *Camel*.

A succession of intermittent calls were made by a variety of passenger ships in 1945/6. People as well as ships had been scattered worldwide and were now anxious to return home. In addition Europe experienced a massive exodus – the last great migration to South Africa, Canada, Australia and New Zealand, as the war weary and refugees alike sought a fresh start in the Dominions. Passenger berths aboard serviceable ships were therefore at a premium.

On 27 June 1945 the *Camel* was pressed into tendering service again, when the 20,000 ton *John Ericsson* made the first peacetime call from New York, landing 110 passengers. Originally built as the Swedish-America Line's *Kungsholm*, the *John Ericsson* was serving as a U.S. Government transport managed by United States Lines. In 1947 she was sold to Home Lines and during the 1950s

British Iron & Steel Corporation (Salvage) Ltd. During the next month she was allocated to Demmelweek & Redding for scrapping and was duly dismantled on Marrowbone Slip in Sutton Harbour.

After the war the waiting rooms at Millbay Pier needed to be redecorated and refurnished. The roof, having been damaged during the 'Blitz', was re-covered with corrugated roofing sheets – a poor substitute for the former slate roof. On 16 September 1955 the Princess Royal Pier's pontoon was replaced at a cost of £70,000. The new pontoon measured 250 x 50 feet. The old pontoon was hulked against East Quay, above Trinity Pier, where, at the time of writing, the remains can still be seen.

The need for post war rationalisation by the shipping lines, together with nationalisation of the railways and their docks, resulted in a major loss of liner trade at Millbay. The Western Region (ex-GWR) and the Southern Region (ex-Southern Railway, largely based on the L&SWR) of British Railways perpetuated many of their pre-nationalisation characteristics. Officially however competition no longer existed. Southampton Docks was rightly promoted as Britain's foremost liner terminal, but at the expense of Millbay's status as a port-of-call. Cunard, P&O, Orient, United States Lines and the NZSCo, each withdrew their Plymouth call. The German lines revived once again, but made no further calls at Plymouth. Some American schemes proposed using Plymouth as a terminus port, to cut the crossing time to a minimum, but in retrospect, a number of the ideas promoted both before and after the war, to compete against the threat of airliners, appear rather fanciful.

THE POST-WAR LINER TRADE

The rationale for disembarking at Plymouth was to conclude the journey as quickly as possible. Liners frequently arrived in the night or during the early hours and departed, largely unnoticed, often long before the city awoke. With the exception of the glamorous CGT liners, the majority of Plymouth's post war line calls were made by combination liners (passenger/cargo liners) which attracted little attention from daytime strollers and bathers on the Hoe and sea front. The liner trade therefore was

low-key compared to halcyon years between the wars, but Plymouth's strategic position in the English Channel continued to serve post war lines – although the nature of the passenger trade had, once again, changed.

A total of 66 liners in 1947 landed 112,996 mailbags and embarked/disembarked 3,589 passengers. 1948 saw largest annual number of mailbags to date – 355,366. Even this was surpassed in the following year when 437,295 mailbags were landed – the all time record at Millbay. Passenger numbers reached a healthy post war peak of 29,038 in 1955, the year which also witnessed the largest post war total of 187 liner calls. Mailbag figures had, however, plummeted to just 39,552 by this time – almost all new mail contracts were being awarded to air-

Top: The waiting rooms were refurbished after the war. Little was altered in the refreshment bar other than provision of tube lighting. This picture was taken just after redecoration was completed. The main waiting room entrance doors at the end of the refreshment bar open out onto Millbay Pier.

Bottom: In the waiting room itself new roof trusses and the underside of the new corrugated roof are evident. New furniture was provided, although the mix of styles suggests previous use.
ASSOCIATED BRITISH PORTS, MILLBAY

The SIR JOHN HAWKINS is pictured at Princess Royal pontoon during the late 1940s. She received her wheelhouse after the 'GRENVILLE was fitted with one. Both were added just after their post war refits and return to service. The 'DRAKE kept her Admiralty fitted wheelhouse until she was broken up.

A. KITTRIDGE COLLECTION

The SIR RICHARD GRENVILLE at Princess Royal Pier in the 1950s..

WORLD SHIP SOCIETY

lines. There was a big increase in the number of private cars meeting passengers at Millbay. The access road from Great Western Road to Millbay Pier was regularly filled with waiting vehicles when a liner called and at times stretched around Great Western Road to Grand Parade. Ironically, whilst the convenience of motor cars enhanced the attraction of the port-of-call, the resulting drain of passengers from the railway was amongst the contributing factors in the declining viability of the liner trade at Plymouth.

TRANS-ATLANTIC LINES

CGT remained as the only pre-war trans-Atlantic line to continue calling at Plymouth. The company's liner *De Grasse*, having been sunk at Bordeaux by the retreating Germans, was salvaged, refitted and in 1947 re-opened CGT's New York service. She made CGT's first post war eastbound call at Plymouth on 22 February 1948, with the *Sir Richard Grenville* attending. The *Ile de France* had served during the war as troopship for the Allies. She was released from war service in April 1947 and underwent virtual rebuilding at the Penhoët shipyard. The *Ile de France* emerged as two funnelled liner and re-entered trans-Atlantic service on 21 July 1949. NDL's *Europa* was ceded to CGT in 1946 and renamed the *Liberté*. In August 1950, after a major refit reportedly costing £7 million, the *Liberté* joined the *Ile de France* and *De Grasse* on the Havre-Southampton-New

During the winter 1953/54 the SIR FRANCIS DRAKE was laid-up in the Inner Basin. During her post war refit the huge towing bar in the stern was removed. She was offered for sale in April 1954. Sold for scrap, the 'DRAKE was broken-up on Marrowbone Slip in Sutton Harbour.

WORLD SHIP SOCIETY

York service, with a Plymouth call eastbound.

The *Flandre* and the *Antilles* were liners of 20,000 tons – intended for CGT's West Indies service. When completed in 1952 the *Flandre* replaced the *De Grasse* on the New York run, while the *Antilles* joined the *Colombie* and was used as planned on the West Indies service, calling at Vigo, San Juan (Puerto Rico), Pointe à Pitre (Guadeloupe), Fort de France (Martinique), La Guaira (Venezuela), Trinidad and Barbados, with an eastbound call at Plymouth. CGT provided the foundation upon which Millbay's post war liner trade was built. Until the end of 1961 hardly a week passed without at least two calls by CGT liners. Passenger numbers landed at Plymouth from both services averaged 200 per call. Mailbags from the New York ships also averaged around 200 per call.

On 13 November 1958 a new daily air service was inaugurated by BOAC between London and New York. The airline's Comet IVs reached New York in just over six hours.

Three days later the *Ile de France* made her last Plymouth call before proceeding to Le Havre and withdrawal from service. She landed 65 passengers and 572 mailbags at Plymouth. It was hoped that she might still be saved from scrapping and re-enter service in the following spring. Her farewell call at Plymouth therefore lacked finality and was largely overlooked. As a result the famous liner's passing barely prompted a mention in the local press.

Home Lines (Panamanian Lines until 1952) started a Hamburg–Channel Ports–Halifax–New York service in 1951 with the *Homeland*, under HAPAG management, calling at Plymouth eastbound. In the following year the company's *Italia* (ex-*John Ericsson*), also managed by HAPAG, started running on the same route. On a typical call in September 1955 she landed 101 passengers at Plymouth before proceeding to Havre and Hamburg. For two years, from 1952, Home Line's *Atlantic* (ex-*Matsonia* of 1927) ran to Quebec from Southampton, calling at Plymouth eastbound. The *Homeric* (ex-

Rebuilt after the war, the ILE DE FRANCE returned to service in July 1949. Incorporated in her refurbished decor were some bronze decorations from the ill-fated NORMANDIE. Her three funnels were replaced by two larger ones. The ILE DE FRANCE was the most glamorous post-war liner to call at Plymouth. There seemed to be an aura about the ship – a sense of occasion each time she called – which set her apart from the larger LIBERTÉ.

ASSOCIATED BRITISH PORTS
COLLECTION
SOUTHAMPTON CITY MUSEUMS

Mariposa of 1931) started a service from Cuxhaven to Le Havre– Southampton–Quebec and Montreal in May 1955, calling at Plymouth on the return voyage. The *Ascania*, a Grimaldi-Siosa liner, called eastbound from Canada on 1 December 1955. It was listed as a Home Lines call, the liner presumably being on charter while the *Homeric* provided her regular winter cruises from New York to the West Indies. All of Home Lines' Plymouth calls were withdrawn by 1960 and the line withdrew completely from the trans-Atlantic trade in 1963.

The Incres Compañia de Navegacion (Incres Line) inaugurated an Antwerp–Plymouth–New York service on 5 July 1950 with the Panamanian registered *Europa* (ex-P&O *Mongolia* of 1922 / ex-NZSCo *Rimutaka*). She was converted to a cruise ship in 1952. In the same year the Incres Line chartered the *Protea* to undertake three voyages between Antwerp, Plymouth and Montreal. The *Protea* was then purchased by the Compañia Internacional Transportadora (Arosa Line) and re-named the *Arosa Kulm*. She was refitted to carry 461 in first class and 919 in tourist dormitories. In March 1952 she commenced running Bremerhaven–Southampton–Montreal/ Quebec, with a return Plymouth call. In the winter months the Arosa Line offered a West Indies service with the *Arosa Kulm*. The *Protea/Arosa Kulm* was no stranger to Plymouth as, between the wars, she had been the American Merchant Line's *American Banker*, being the only AML ship to have survived the Second World War. The *Arosa Star* (ex-*Puerto Rico*), *Arosa Sun* (ex-*Felix Roussel*),

and the *Arosa Sky* (ex-*La Marseillaise*) entered service for the Arosa Line in 1954, 1955 and 1957 respectively. Each ran from Channel Ports to New York or Canada, with eastbound Plymouth calls.

The Arosa Line was in financial difficulties by 1958 and in December of the same year the *Arosa Kulm* was arrested at Plymouth by the Admiralty Marshal, for failure of her owners to meet certain payments. 70 Jamaican passengers aboard had booked for Southampton and there were angry scenes when they learned the rail fare to London. They refused to buy tickets from the British Railways ticket clerks who went out on the tender and the situation was only resolved when Bellamy & Co. (Plymouth) Ltd, agents for the Arosa Line, paid the difference in the train fare to London. The *Arosa Kulm* remained at Plymouth until 18 December when she was moved to Fowey pending an auction for scrap.

The Oranje Lijn Maatschappij Zeetransport N.V. (Oranje Line) commissioned the *Prins Willem Van Oranje* in 1953, running from Rotterdam, Southampton and/or Plymouth to Montreal. The number of passengers embarking at Plymouth was small, but the *Prins Willem Van Oranje* was a regular caller until the late '50s. When the St Lawrence Seaway opened in 1959 the Oranje Line introduced two new combination liners, the *Prinses Irene* and in 1961 the *Prinses Margriet*. Both ships made westbound calls at Plymouth.

COLONIAL AND OTHER LINES

There was a notable increase in passenger line calls from the West Indies in the 1950s. After the war there was much unemployment and hardship in the islands. Conversely Britain needed to increase its labour force to meet the immediate demands of post war reconstruction. Thus, after a century of emigration, Plymouth now witnessed a short period of immigration. Thousands of West Indians landed at Plymouth to seek employment in Britain's industrial centres.

Dutch lines on West Indies routes were regular post war callers at Plymouth. KNSM ships on the old KWIM routes continued to call at Plymouth eastbound. Early callers

The PRINS WILLEM VAN ORANJE of the Oranje Lijn (Mij. Zeetransport) N.V.
A. KITTRIDGE COLLECTION

included the *Boskoop* – one of the company's pre-war combination liners, the *Bonaire* – an ex-German ship which had been managed by KNSM for the Dutch Government since 1940, and the *Cottica* – a pre-war caller at Plymouth. Two other ships which entered the service after the war were the *Orangjestad* and *Willemstad*. These were originally the KNSM cargo ships *Pericles* and *Socrates*, both of which had called at Plymouth before the war. Each ship was converted to carry 94 first class passengers, with additional dormitory accommodation if required. Their route was Amsterdam, Southampton, Madeira, Pointe à Pitre, Fort de France, Barbados, Trinidad, Paramaribo and Georgetown. The return trip called at Plymouth before proceeding to Amsterdam. Passengers landing at Plymouth averaged around 40, but doubled when West Indian immigrants were landed. Mail ranged anywhere between 5 to 200 bags. In 1957 two new KNSM liners entered West Indies service. The *Oranje Nassau* and *Prins der Nederlanden* were 7,200 ton combination liners, with a capacity for 116 first class passengers and 68 in dormitory accommodation. Both made regular east-bound calls at Plymouth. Dormitory or group accommodation was the 1950's equivalent of the old steerage class and was introduced as migrant accommodation by some post war West Indies lines.

There were a number of charter calls from the West Indies, including the Sitmar Line's *Fairsea*, which called on 21 March 1955 to land 661 passengers. The *Auriga* of the Grimaldi Line also called in March 1955 with passengers from the West Indies. The *Auriga* was originally registered at Plymouth in 1909 as the *Ruahine* of the NZSCo. The *Jamaica Producer* and the *Jamaica Planter* of the Jamaica Direct Fruit Line made occasional calls, but they only accommodated twelve passengers.

The trans-Atlantic liners of NASM did not resume calls, but the company's combination liners *Dalerdyk*, *Dongedyk* and *Diemerdyk* did inaugurate a Plymouth call, westbound, on their service to the Caribbean, Panama Canal, Los Angeles, San Francisco, Portland, Seattle, Victoria and Vancouver. They were joined later in 1957 by another combination liner, the *Dinteldyk*. The ships rarely embarked more than thirty passengers at Plymouth.

The Blue Star Line's entire passenger fleet was sunk by U-boats during the war. In 1947–8 four new 10,800 ton combination liners were built to replace the company's losses. Named the *Argentina Star, Brasil Star, Uruguay Star* and *Paraguay Star*, they carried 53 first class passengers. From London and Channel ports the liners ran to Rio de Janeiro, Santos, Montevideo and Buenos Aires. A Plymouth call was made on some outward bound voyages.

The PSNCo. liners – *Reina del Pacifico* and *Reina del Mar* – made occasional calls eastbound. When the *Reina del Pacifico* called on 8 September 1955 she landed 185 passengers and 240 mailbags. She was withdrawn from service in 1958.

Ellerman & Bucknall liners on the South African route continued to call after the war. Initially the service was maintained by pre-war vessels including the *City of Paris* and *City of Nagpur*. When the *City of Paris* called at Plymouth on 27 September 1955 she landed

113 passengers. Between 1952 and 1954 four new 13,300 ton combination liners were built for the line. The *City of Port Elizabeth, City of Exeter, City of York* and *City of Durban* carried 107 passengers in first class only. From London and Channel ports the ships ran to Cape Town and up the east Africa coast to Beira. A home bound call was made at Plymouth, landing up to 80 passengers at times.

An ambulance awaited the *City of Port Elizabeth* on one call in 1959. Two passengers had sustained injuries when the ship ran into a heavy gale near Las Palmas. There had been eight casualties and of the two injured passengers taken off one had suffered severe concussion, the other fractured ribs. 51 passengers were landed on this occasion.

Liners from the Round Africa service of the Union-Castle line maintained a call until the route closed in 1961. The service was twice monthly, with a ship travelling in each direction around Africa. Liners included the *Braemar*

Launched for the Pacific Steam Navigation Company in 1955, the 20,000 ton REINA DEL MAR entered service in the following year – running from Liverpool to Valparaiso via the Panama Canal. She is pictured in Plymouth Sound with the SIR JOHN HAWKINS in attendance. Two smaller vessels are moored alongside the tender, the nearest being the Port Health Authority's launch, the ARGUS. Photographed from Jennycliff, the lens has foreshortened the distance between the Sound and Cawsand Bay in the background.

SYDNEY GOODMAN COLLECTION

Castle, Rhodesia Castle, Warwick Castle, D[...]
Castle and *Dunnottar Castle*. Some home-b[...]
calls were made at Plymouth.

BI continued briefly to call home-bou[...]
their East African service with the *Mo[...]*
Matiana, and *Mantola*. All of these ships [...]
withdrawn by 1954 and the call ceased. In [...]
BI started educational cruises with the *De[...]*
(ex-*Devonshire* of the Bibby Line). The *De[...]*
subsequently made calls at Plymouth to em[...]
and disembark school children.

Since 1919 P&O held the majority s[...]
holding of the Orient Line. From 1960 [...]
1966 the companies adopted the title [...]
Orient. It was in this guise that some h[...]
bound calls from Australia were made b[...]
Orion and *Iberia* in the early '60s.

One of the most regular post-war calle[...]
the winter months at least, was the Be[...]
Line's *Venus*. The 6,270 ton motorship was [...]
in 1931 for the Bergen Line's Newca[...]
Bergen service. During the winter she operated
a passenger service from Bergen to Madeira
and Tenerife, with a Plymouth call in each
direction. The number of passengers joining
and leaving the ship at Plymouth numbered
well over 200 at times. As the frequency of her
calls were at three day (from Bergen) and six
day (from Madeira) intervals, the ship generated a very healthy trade for Millbay.

country, but this was of no consolation to the
passengers and crew of the *Venus*, which ran
aground on a rock ledge, 100 yards from
Mount Batten. Passengers were taken off and
tugs attempted, unsuccessfully, to pull the ship
free. The RAF, from Mount Batten, played
searchlights on the ship all night and a second
attempt to pull the liner off the rocks failed.
Crowds gathered on Plymouth Hoe and at

Passengers head out to embark aboard the twin funnelled VENUS *and the Blue Star Line's* URUGUAY STAR *(centre) – both outward bound to Madeira and South America respectively. On the right is either the* DURBAN CASTLE *or* WARWICK CASTLE, *homeward-bound on the Union-Castle's Round Africa service.*
COURTESY
WESTERN MORNING NEWS

LINE

Throughout the second half of the 1950s liner trade declined irrevocably. There over 170 calls in 1958, but in the following year the number was reduced to 113. Withdrawal of calls by the Arosa and Home lines each contributed to the drop. In 1960 the figure fell to just 93 liner calls, providing 12,345 passengers and only 8,103 mailbags.

By the late 1950s some 120,000 immigrants had arrived in the UK, many travelling by sea

GRENVILLE (nearest) and SIR JOHN HAWKINS, and the Port Health Authority launch ARGUS, are moored at Princess Royal Pier pontoon. A railway carriage can be seen at the buffer stops on East Quay.

IVOR IRELAND

the rocks, the *Venus* was finally pulled free. She was taken to West Wharf in Millbay Docks and de-stored pending dry docking in Devonport Dockyard, where she was towed on the 29th. She was replaced by Bergen Line's *Meteor*, but returned to the service later in 1955.

and landing at Tilbury, Liverpool and Plymouth. R. A. Butler's Immigration Bill of 1961 sought to control the flow of Commonwealth immigrants resulting in an end to calls by immigrant liners at Plymouth. Then, later in 1961, came the fatal blow with CGT's announcement of the closure of its Plymouth call.

As CGT's new 66,000 ton super-liner, the *France*, neared completion at the Penhoët Yard, St. Nazaire, the *Liberté* was withdrawn from service. She made her final voyage in November 1961, calling in at Plymouth for the last time on 16 November. The Lord Mayor of Plymouth, Sir Arthur Goldberg, went aboard and received from the liner's master, Capt. Charles Ferrenbach, a bronze medal depicting the ship and the figure of Liberté. Capt. Ferrenbach said that he had been sailing into Plymouth ever since 1928, when he was a midshipman aboard the *Ile de France*, but he had never had

the opportunity to step ashore. The Lord Mayor duly invited him to return to Plymouth in the future as a guest of the city. With three prolonged, deep blasts from her steam whistles the *Liberté* signalled farewell and she slipped out of Cawsand Bay – the last trans-Atlantic leviathan that Plymouth would see.

CGT indicated that in future their only British calls would be made at Southampton. G. Haswell & Co., CGT's Plymouth agents, retained a Plymouth office but their headquarters were moved to Southampton. Mr F. G. Dean, British Rail's district traffic superintendent, stated that such had been the decline in liner traffic that one of the tenders would have to go. In March 1962 the *Sir John Hawkins* was laid up in the Inner Basin and offered for sale. She was sold two months later to Scheepswerf-en-Machine Handel, N.V., Holland, for breaking. On 26 May at 10.45pm the *'Hawkins* left

The last trans-Atlantic super-liner to call at Plymouth, the LIBERTÉ, *pictured anchored in Cawsand Bay. This spectacular ship – the fourth largest liner in the world at the time – had called occasionally as NDL's* EUROPA *before the war. As the* LIBERTÉ *she was a regular caller from the time she entered service in 1950 until she made her final Plymouth call on 16 November 1961.*

COURTESY
WESTERN MORNING NEWS

Pictured in January 1961 the SIR JOHN HAWKINS approaches Millbay Pier. The photograph illustrates well the tremendous flare of the bows and the ample width of the ship. The withdrawal of CGT's calls at the end of 1961 signalled the end for the 33 year old tender.
ASSOCIATED BRITISH PORTS, MILLBAY

The SIR JOHN HAWKINS laid-up amongst weathering timber in the Inner Basin between March – May 1962.
MICHAEL DOHERTY

Millbay *en-route* to the breaker's yard in Ostend.

There were only 82 line calls at Plymouth in 1962, providing 6,425 passengers and 2,872 mailbags. Conversely, Southampton handled 76 liner movements in November alone, many of them terminus dockings. The *Sir Richard Grenville* attended calls by KNSM and NASM, which although regular Plymouth callers, were providing such small numbers that their disembarking passengers were regularly outnumbered by the *'Grenville*'s crew.

A report by the Plymouth & District Trades Council in May 1962 suggested that the Admiralty should be approached regarding the use of South Yard in Devonport Dockyard as a liner terminal. The report continued:

> ...Millbay Docks were fully equipped to handle passengers when they were modernised some years ago. These facilities are being thrown away because dredging and other work required to enable liners to get into Millbay has not been undertaken.

It was further noted in the report that one shipping company had indicated its interest in switching to Plymouth because of poor labour relations at Southampton. This latter point was rather opportunist, as two days prior to the report's publication P&O-Orient's *Orion* had been diverted to Plymouth due to a strike at Southampton. On the evening of 17 May the Royal Rotterdam Lloyd Line's *Willem Ruys* arrived at Plymouth, having also been diverted because of the strike. She spent the night in Plymouth Sound and the *Sir Richard Grenville* made a start that evening in unloading 1,200 pieces of cabin luggage, 400 pieces of heavy luggage and 535 mailbags. In the morning 618 passengers and four cars were disembarked. British Rail laid on two 12 coach trains complete with dining cars. The call revived memories of better days, but the *'Grenville* had a busy time attending the liner alone.

Mr. B. Richards, the Dock Manager said that 'Any ships offered to Plymouth are always seriously considered. We make every effort to work them'. Any optimism was dashed on the following day when the Southampton dock workers voted for a return to work. To compound the disappointment felt at Millbay, on the same day the

Meteor made the Bergen Line's last Plymouth call. The *Brasil Star*'s call on 17 August proved to be the Blue Star Line's final visit. The Oranje Line announced its intention to close its passenger service to Canada in the summer of 1963.

CLOSURE AS A PORT-OF-CALL FOR LINERS

Providing that losses incurred in the operation of tenders at Millbay could be recouped by the additional railway revenue they generated, their position was secure. But the *Sir Richard Grenville* had shown a deficit of £23,000 in 1962, which was nowhere near being offset by rail revenue. As the expected total of line calls for 1963 was only 54, it was announced that Millbay's liner passenger facilities would be closed at the end of October.

To add to the problems at Millbay, the tenders' local excursion trade had also been in terminal decline since the mid '50s. On 9 August 1963 the *'Grenville* made what was intended to be her last excursion to the Eddystone, 150 passengers had to be turned away as she was filled to capacity. On reaching the Eddystone, Capt. C. F. Foxwell of the *'Grenville* sounded the whistle, and in time honoured fashion the lighthouse keepers waved in reply. The trip was specially organised by the Plymouth Chamber of Commerce, as public excursions had ended when the *Sir John Hawkins* was withdrawn in the previous year. On Wednesday 4 September

The SIR RICHARD GRENVILLE's first farewell cruise to the Eddystone on 9 August 1963.
MICHAEL DOHERTY

an extra excursion was organised by four local businessmen. Unfortunately steady rain discouraged passengers and only 200 joined the tender. At the end of the trip they all joined in singing Auld Lang Syne.

KNSM's *Oranje Nassau* called on 7 September and landed 35 passengers and 31 mailbags. On 16 September BI's educational cruise ship, the *Devonia* embarked 950 schoolchildren and their accompanying adults. Two days later KNSM's *Oranjestad* made her last call. NASM's *Dongedyk* and *Dinteldyk* made their final calls on 20 and 26 September respectively. On the 27th Ellerman & Bucknall's *City of Port Elizabeth* landed 48 passengers and 5 cars. Railway carriages were laid on at Millbay

In December 1963 the SIR RICHARD GRENVILLE was purchased by Guernsey Lines Ltd. She was renamed LA DUCHESSE DE NORMANDIE and maintained summer services between the Channel Islands and ports in Northern France. She is pictured in October 1966 in Millbay's Dry Dock. On the right are Willoughby's workshops. This was the ex-tender's penultimate visit to Plymouth – for maintenance work by Willoughby's. When Jersey Lines went into liquidation in 1969 LA DUCHESSE DE NORMANDIE was laid up at Millbay until sold for scrap later in the year. The Dry Dock was infilled in the early 1970s and now forms a part of the vehicle marshalling area for Brittany Ferries.
SYDNEY GOODMAN COLLECTION

The former ocean passenger and mail facilities at Millbay in the late 1960s. Gone are the tenders, Princess Royal Pier pontoon and the passenger trains. The Waiting Room and baggage handling sheds are closed. The mail conveyor survives, disused, a while longer. The Port Health Authority's launch remains in use, moored at Princess Royal Pier. Behind the warehouses the houses of Garden Crescent back onto Great Western Road. At the end of Millbay Pier is the signal mast with two warning balls hoisted – indicating that a vessel is about to depart from the docks. One ball signalled an incoming vessel. The photograph was taken from the top of the grain silo on West Wharf.

ASSOCIATED BRITISH PORTS, MILLBAY

for the Ellerman liner's passengers to join the 10.30am Paddington train at North Road. This was the last Ellerman & Bucknall call, and the last liner handled at Plymouth by Haswell & Co. On 30 September the *Devonia* returned to disembark her cruise passengers. Nearly 1,000 were landed, representing one of the largest, if not the largest, disembarkations by tender for Millbay. The *Devonia's* departure ended BI's long association with the passenger trade of the port.

Miss Joan Vickers, M.P. for Devonport, made some well meaning, but naïve, efforts to secure the future of the *Sir Richard Grenville*. She felt that the costs of running the tender might be reduced by running from the Inner Basin! She thought that excursions had been

insufficiently advertised in the past and wrote to Ernest Marples, Minister of Transport, setting out these points. She also wrote to Dr Beeching, Chairman of British Rail, suggesting that the tender could be retained for taking children out to educational cruise ships. The General Manager of BR Western Region diplomatically replied that there was nothing to prevent anybody from acquiring the tender at the end of October.

The penultimate liner call was made on 6 October 1963 by KNSM's *Prins der Nederlanden*. She landed 12 passengers and 215 mailbags, the last mails to be handled at Millbay. Efforts were being made to attract alternative business for Millbay Docks. On 16 October Bernard Richards the Dock Manager,

The Millbay Pier area in 1988, soon after demolition had commenced. All buildings on the pier, except the white harbour offices, have been demolished, revealing a view of Jennycliff, Staddon Heights and Plymouth Sound that had been obscured since the 1850s. On Princess Royal Pier the Plymouth Lifeboat station has been vacated – removed temporarily to Sutton Harbour. On East Quay the Pier Hotel building and the five warehouses remain standing – but only for a few weeks longer. On the far left are the remains of the railway station awning.

A. KITTRIDGE

returned from a five day visit to Brittany, where calls were made to agents in Brest, Roscoff and Morlaix. Talks had been held with produce exporters with a view to expanding trade. With Mr. Richards' delegation were C. A. Brindle, Marketing Manager for British Rail Plymouth and R. Vosper of Bellamy & Co. (Plymouth) Ltd. This trade mission would result ultimately in establishing Millbay as the first British ferry port for the French cross channel ferry company – Brittany Ferries.

Plymouth's last liner call passed virtually unnoticed. At midnight on 18/19 October NASM's *Diemerdyk* claimed the distinction of being the last liner to be attended by the *Sir Richard Grenville*. The Dutch liner embarked 18 passengers and one car. The *'Grenville* returned, empty, in the dead of night to a deserted Millbay Pier and awaited the official closure on 31 October. When she was subsequently transferred to a lay up berth in the Inner Basin a stillness fell over Millbay Pier. Gangways, crowd barriers and steps for boarding the trains lay redundant where they had last been used. The booking office window in the Customs Office and the waiting room doors of the Pier Hotel building were shut. The blackboard, upon which which was announced the next liner call, remained blank. Plymouth's 113 year role as a mail port had ended.

MILLBAY PIER

For a quarter of a century the buildings and piers which made up the former ocean passenger and mails facility played host to a variety of tenants and businesses. The Pier Hotel building housed an electrical showroom. The Plymouth Lifeboat Station, formerly sited in the outer basin, near the lock gates, was moved to a more convenient location at Princess Royal Pier. Tenders of the Royal Maritime Auxiliary Service, usually attending ships of the Royal Fleet Auxiliary in the Sound, landed personnel on Princess Royal Pier – recalling the days when hundreds of naval ratings of many nationalities regularly stepped ashore from liberty boats at Millbay Pier. The RMAS landing has since been moved to its own pontoon, on the north side of Trinity Pier.

Perhaps only to those who recalled the liner trade, Millbay Pier became a melancholy place. Unlike Princess Royal and Trinity Piers, no fixed role ever seemed to be found for it. Fully exposed to the elements when the awning was removed the buildings slowly deteriorated and went out of use. Demolition of warehouses 1–5 and the buildings on Millbay Pier began in 1988. On 9 December of the same year Dr David Owen, MP for Devonport, laid a commemorative roof ridge-tile to mark the completion of the showhouse of Millbay Marina Village. The development now occupies the

The deserted Pier Hotel building in 1988, with Bellamy & Co's sign still above the door – the company moved to premises in the Ferryport building on the north west side of the docks. The door on the side, to the right, was once the main entrance to the Waiting Rooms.

A. KITTRIDGE

The Pier Hotel building demolished in March 1989. Exposed to view is the tiled wall of the Refreshment Bar and one of the cast iron pillars. Wightwick's Customs Office alone amongst the former passenger/mail buildings escaped destruction, owing to its architectural importance.

A. KITTRIDGE

Very few traces remain to indicate Ocean Quay's former use. One surprising survivor is this Southern Railway cast iron notice which is located alongside the one time station/pier master's house in Richmond Walk.

Far right: The last section of rail of the Stonehouse Pool Branch emerges from the limestone quarry, crosses Richmond Walk on the level and now terminates at a wall on the opposite side of the road.

A. KITTRIDGE

whole of the former ocean liner facility and comprises 90 properties with pontoon marina berths. The Pier Hotel building of 1850 was demolished in March 1989 and within two years the first stage of the marina was complete. Only Wightwick's attractive, limestone Customs Office of 1850 has survived. A Grade II listed building, the Customs Office has been renovated and converted as a shore–base for the Plymouth Lifeboat, which now operates from adjacent moorings in the marina. The stone abutment of the Princess Royal Pier supports the bridge to the marina's pontoons. Three mosaics at Princess Royal pier head draw largely upon local myth to commemorate

Millbay's past history. A second phase of the marina development is proposed and will extend to include the area of dock from Trinity Pier to Clyde Quay – the whole of the eastern side of the dock.

The passenger/mail facility at Millbay has been consigned to history, but today Millbay Docks handles more passengers than ever before – Channel ferries having replaced the ocean liners and tenders. It is also satisfying to note that cruise ships continue the long tradition of ocean passenger ship calls at Plymouth – albeit in greatly reduced numbers compared to the line calls that Plymouth once enjoyed for over a century.

HAPAG-Lloyd's 37,000 ton cruise ship, the EUROPA, at anchor in Plymouth Sound on 28 September 1991. A descendant of the famous trans-Atlantic liners of HAPAG and Norddeutscher Lloyd, she is one of a number of cruise ships which make seasonal calls at Plymouth today.

A. KITTRIDGE

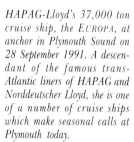

ACKNOWLEDGEMENTS & SOURCES

This history is the culmination of the author's researches over a number of years, but the resulting book would have been inferior without the generous assistance of correspondents and friends. Foremost in the latter category I owe a debt of gratitude to Douglass B. Hoppins, who, fortunately for the both the author and the reader, made contact relatively early in my research for this book. Douglass offered free access to both his and his father's – the late D. G. Hoppins – photographic collections, which include many original prints of official GWR photographs. Douglass also provided a copy of his father's typescript, *Some Notes on the History of the Great Western Docks at Millbay, 1840–1932* (compiled 1932–3, amended 1943–6). He catalogued the Millbay section of the Associated British Ports photographic collection for the Tudor House Museum, Southampton and supplied a copy of the resulting list. Finally I am grateful for Douglass' meticulous reading of my final manuscript.

Michael Doherty and Bernard Mills lent a copy of their account of the history of the liner tenders at Plymouth. The late Geoffrey Grimshaw offered copies of his immediate post war notes and correspondence regarding the tenders at Plymouth, which he researched for his book *British Pleasure Steamers 1920–1939*, Richard Tilling 1945. J. G. Hosegood provided information additional to his book *Great Western Travelling Post Offices*. J. D. Lutterot (ex-Chief Radio Officer KNSM) responded to a request for assistance and provided otherwise elusive information about KWIM and KNSM. Alastair W. McRobb supplied information regarding the activities of the tenders at Scapa Flow during the Second World War. Keith Perkins provided some of his original research material relating to James Meadows Rendel which was used in Michael R. Lane's book *The Rendel Connection*, Quiller Press 1989. R. Smaldon of Bellamy & Co. (Plymouth) Ltd. supplied records of the final liner calls in 1963 and provided a history of Bellamy & Co. (Plymouth) Ltd. – which was originally prepared in 1979 for the bi-centennial of the company's origins.

E. Chapman, Docks Manager and Jane Cridall, Associated British Ports, Millbay, made available the dock's photographic collection. Sydney Goodman lent prints from his huge Plymouth and Naval photographic collection. Nigel Overton, ex-Keeper of Maritime & Aviation History for The Tudor House Museum, Southampton supplied prints from the museum's Associated British Ports photographic collection. Other photographs were loaned or supplied by Sarah Ackrill, British Railways, Michael Doherty, Ivor Ireland, Brian Jackson, the late Jack Kingston, National Maritime Museum, Post Office Museum, *Western Morning News* and the World Ship Society. The author and publisher have attempted to ascertain the provenance of each photograph in the book and apologise if they have inadvertently infringed copyright.

Sources:

At Plymouth Reference Library research has been conducted into the microfilm archives of the *Western Daily Mercury*, *Western Morning News* and *Western Evening Herald*. Particular reference was made to the Shipping Intelligence column of the *Western Morning News*, which, until 1939, listed all mailboat calls and provided details of each ship's voyage, passenger numbers and mail quantities.

Reference has also been made to a number of publications and documents held in the Local History Library at Plymouth, including Plymouth Chamber of Commerce reports and *Kelly's Directories*.

Newspapers, magazines and directories:

Great Western Magazine
Sea Breezes
The Shipping World Year Book and
    Port Directory of the World
Ships Monthly
Ward Lock & Co's Guide Books for Plymouth &
    South West Devon
Western Daily Mercury
Western Evening Herald
Western Morning News

Articles:

Bryant, W.N. 'Plymouth Emigration Depot in the Nineteenth Century' *Devon & Cornwall Notes & Queries* Vol. 36 part 4.

Bibliography:

Barnett, C. *Engage The Enemy More Closely (The Royal Navy in the Second World War)*, Hodder & Staughton 1991.

Barry, J. *Flying the North Atlantic*, Batsford 1987.

Bonsor, N. R. P. *North Atlantic Seaway*, T. Stephenson & Sons 1955.

Bonsor, N. R. P. *South Atlantic Seaway*, Brookside Publications 1983.

Cooke, A. *Emigrant Ships*, Carmania Press 1991.

Cowden, J. E. and Duffy, J. O. C. *The Elder Dempster Fleet History 1852 – 1985*, Mallett & Bell Publications 1986.

Duckworth, C. L. D. and Langmuir, G. E. *Railway and Other Steamers*. T. Stephenson & Sons 1968.

Farr, G. *West Country Passenger Steamers*. T. Stephenson & Sons 1967.

Gaskell Brown, C. (Editor) *A Guide to the Industrial Archaeology of Plymouth and Millbrook*. Plymouth City Museum and WEA 1980.

Gill, C. *Mailboats* – typescript. Plymouth Local History Library.

Gill, C. *Plymouth: A New History, Volume Two*. David & Charles 1979.

Gill, C. *Sutton Harbour*. Sutton Harbour Improvement Company 1970.

Haws, D. *British India S. N. Co.*, TCL Publications 1987.

Haws, D. *Shaw, Savill & Albion*, TCL Publications 1987.

Haws, D. *Union, Castle and Union-Castle Lines*, TCL Publications 1990.

Hosegood, J. G. *Great Western Railway Travelling Post Offices*, Wild Swan Publications 1983.

Hughes, T. *The Blue Riband of the Atlantic*. Patrick Stephens 1973

Lucking, J. H. *The Great Western at Weymouth*. David & Charles 1971.

Lubbock, B. *The Colonial Clippers*, Brown, Son & Ferguson 1975 reprint of 1948 edition.

McCart, N. *Passenger Ships of the Orient Line*, Patrick Stephens 1987.

Miller, W. H. *The Last Atlantic Liners*, Conway Maritime Press 1985.

Miller, W. H. *The Last Blue Water Liners*, Conway Maritime Press 1986.

Mitchell, W. H. and Sawyer, L. A. *The Cape Run*, Lavenham 1987.

Paget-Tomlinson, E. W. *The History of the Bibby Line*, Bibby Line Ltd. 1970.

Rabson, S. & O'Donoghue, K. *P&O A Fleet History*, World Ship Society 1988.

Russell, J. H. *A Pictorial Record of Great Western Coaches (Parts One and Two)*. Oxford Publishing 1972/3.

Savill, D. *Sail to New Zealand*, Robert Hale 1986.

Savill, D. and Haws, D. *Aberdeen and Aberdeen & Commonwealth Lines*, TCL Publications 1989.

Seiler, O. J. *Crossing the Tracks of Columbus*, Verlag E. S. Mittler & Sohn 1992.

INDEX